The Cooking of
Spain
&
Portugal

The Cooking of
Spain & Portugal

Tony Schmaeling

OMEGA BOOKS

ACKNOWLEDGEMENTS

Establishing contacts and arranging itineraries in distant countries is never easy, so that any assistance received is always welcome. In Sydney the commercial consul for Spain, Mr Roberto Cunad provided me with my initial contacts in Spain, while in Madrid, Juan Sanchez Lorenzo, chief of publicity and public relations of the Secretariat of Tourism assisted me in working out detailed plans of restaurants to visit and places to stay. With the enthusiastic help of local tourist authorities, the unstinting co-operation from chefs and restaurant owners, and despite language problems, the tour of Spain was a great success. Helpful people, a beautiful country and delicious food made it a very pleasant experience.

Getting in contact with the Portuguese tourist authorities proved to be more difficult. So, what help I received, I appreciated very much. Roberto de Sausa from the Portuguese National Tourist Office in London gave me a very informative book on his country's cooking. In Lisbon, Miss Fatima in Promocion Turistica and Miss Mensurado, Tourism Manager of the Enatur, whose organisation runs the Pousadas, the government tourist inns, mapped out an interesting itinerary for me. As always, chefs and restaurant owners entered into the spirit of the venture and provided me with recipes and food for photography.

In Sydney Gwen and Michelle Flanders did their best to decipher reams of my illegible longhand and typed it into a neat manuscript.

My editor, Susan Tomnay once more applied her great skill in putting the whole book together.

The original idea of this series of cookbooks on the food of Europe came from Kevin Weldon, at the time Managing Director of Paul Hamlyn. I thank him, Warwick Jacobson, the company's Publishing Manager and Anne Wilson, the Chief Editor for their encouragement and technical support.

I thank Graham Turnbull of Traveland for his company's assistance in my travels through Europe to collect materials for this series. His London office gave me valuable assistance.

David Davis, my camera assistant, was a great help and untiring travel companion.

This edition published 1983 by Omega Books Ltd,
1 West Street, Ware, Hertfordshire, under licence
from the proprietor.

ISBN 0 907853 07 2

Printed and bound in Hong Kong by South China Printing Co.

CONTENTS

SPAIN

PORTUGAL

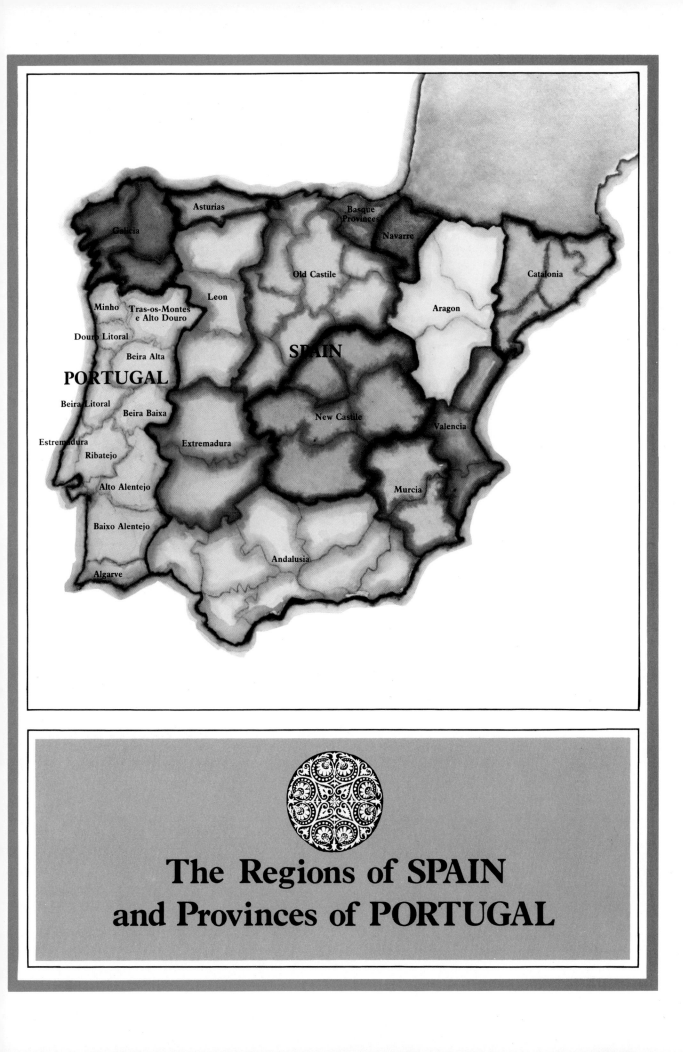

The Regions of SPAIN
and Provinces of PORTUGAL

SPAIN

INTRODUCTION

The Spanish cuisine is the sum total of many different parts. The diversity of its cooking styles makes it fascinating and compelling. A close study is a rewarding task, the price a gourmet's delight, yet simple appreciation of good food is sufficient. Spanish cooking is basically countrymen's fare and at no stage are special skills required to master even the more complex dishes.

I went to Spain with the average person's preconceptions and limited knowledge of what Spanish food is all about.

For years, in summer, I had been enjoying a refreshing and cooling Gazpacho; I even developed my own version of it. In one of Sydney's Spanish restaurants I came across a very plausible Paella. I had tried chorizos and tortilla, and once I partook in an authentically prepared Cochimillo Asado, the roast suckling pig of Old Castile. I adored the fine slivers of Spanish ham, the pinchos, marinated skewers of grilled meat, mushrooms garnished with garlic and parsley, even garlic prawns, without knowing that I was tasting a few of the endless variety of tempting traditional snacks called tapas.

However, these and a few more delights of the Spanish kitchen had sufficiently whetted my appetite and curiosity to send me on my way to find and explore the real thing.

The picture I offer in this book is by no means complete. To do true justice to the cooking in Spain would require a tome more voluminous than the present on each of the thirteen regions of Spain. The project would be further complicated by the fact that most of these regions comprise several provinces, many of which have their individual way of cooking.

I started my journey in Madrid where, in addition to the cooking of its own region (New Castile), one can find the food from all parts of the whole country. I was eager to get underway but I dwelt long enough to try an authentic version of the already-familiar Cochimillo Asado. It was an appropriate beginning, as the central regions of central Spain, New Castile and Old Castile, are renowned for their roasts.

My plan was to collect dishes that were peculiar to each region and town through which I passed. I was not disappointed.

Game and freshwater fish are also specialities of the central provinces, which are good hunting grounds and where rivers yield a good catch. So while in Toledo I tried casseroled partridge, and in the charming mediaeval town of Ávila, trout from the river Tormes was served in an unusual combination with bacon and chorizo sausage.

My road to the north-west took me through the historical town of Salamanca, which rises dramatically above the Tormes with its Roman bridge.

The brown, dusty landscape of the centre soon changes to the moist, misty and vivid green of Galicia. Typically for this part of the country, it rained incessantly. Yet Santiago de Compostela, for a thousand years renowned for its shrine of St James the Apostle, lost none of its theatrical impact. For a part of Spain that has some of the best and most-varied supply of seafood, it is fitting that the symbol of the patron saint should be a scallop shell. Scallops here are the best I have tasted anywhere.

The Basques have the reputation of being the best cooks in Spain, I was therefore not surprised to find in San Sebastián the best restaurant I came across during my stay in that country. Juan Arzac is a great friend and admirer of Michel Guérard, and in his restaurant he prepares an original Nouvelle Cuisine version of traditional Basque cooking.

Pamplona, in Navarre, is well known for the festival of San Fermín when the whole town takes to the street for the running of the bulls.

The cooking of Navarre and of neighbouring Aragon is best known for its sauces. 'A la Chilindrón' denotes a dish served in a sauce that combines garlic, onions, tomatoes, red or green peppers (capsicums) and ham; these ingredients, and the various meats such as rabbit, lamb, chicken or veal with which they are used, blend into a characteristic flavour. There is also a number of peculiar dishes which are called Migas in which breadcrumbs are the main ingredient. Migas a la Pastora, from El Cachirulo in Zaragoza, is a simple mixture of breadcrumbs, garlic, button mushrooms and chorizo – a tasty start to a meal.

I was looking forward to my visit in Barcelona. This time my expectations were not only of a culinary nature. As an architect I had always admired the idiosyncratic buildings of Antonio Gaudí and I was soon to see them in real life. The Catalonian characteristic of original and independent thought is reflected in his work, as it is in the cooking of this region. Gastronomically there is a strong French influence, and dishes here are similar to those across the border. The pungent Ali-oli, which reappears all along the Mediterranean coast of Spain and France, is of Catalán origin.

With all the best of seafood in the Mediterranean, it is natural that specialities of the region are from the sea. Zarzuela de Pescado is a favourite, and there is no better place to taste it than one of the many seafood restaurants of Barceloneta. There is also the Catalán version of the Paella which, surprisingly, does not include fish but combines chicken and snails.

From Barcelona I travelled south past the beaches and holiday resorts which extend along the coast. My next stop was Valencia, in the centre of Spain's rice country. The Valencia region is an important agricultural district and has been so since the prosperous centuries of Moorish domination. Not only did they introduce rice growing, orange groves and almond orchards, but they left behind a sophisticated and efficient irrigation system.

Murcia, the region south of Valencia produces good wines and the Sangria I tasted there was made from local red wine, peach juice, peaches and mineral water.

I wish I had had the opportunity of spending more time in Andalusia. A fleeting visit to Granada and Sevilla gave me a tantalising taste of the most romantic of the Spanish regions. Flamenco music, the singing, dancing and gypsy guitarists, evoke a strong image of Spain. The south has hot summers and winters are short. Regional food is light, and the refreshing Gazpacho is a typical example of food adapted to a hot climate. Most food is fried crisp in good-quality oil.

The last region I visited before travelling to Portugal was Extremadura. As its name implies, it has a severe climate and living conditions in the past have been hard. Local people make the best of what is available and local dishes reflect a frugal approach to life. However, there is good hunting for deer, hare, partridge and even wild boar. Local chorizo is well known for its strong taste.

My short visit to Spain and the brief glimpse of its food has made me determined to return and to savour with leisure the great flavour of its cooking.

All flour is plain (all-purpose) flour unless otherwise specified.

TAPAS AND ENTREMESES

If the visitor to Spain had only one opportunity of trying Spanish food, the choice should be tapas, that infinite variety of delicious snacks offered with sherry and other wines in Spanish tavernas and bars. The range of these dishes encompasses nearly the whole gamut of Spanish food and flavour.

They can be as simple as a morsel of seafood cooked on the grill, a slice of chorizo (a spicy salami-like sausage), pieces of serrano ham, or olives; or as elaborate as stewed quail, various croquettes and pasties, kidneys sautéed in a white wine sauce with onions, peas and sweet red peppers, clams a la marinara, small squid in their own ink, marinated fish and many others.

The word tapa in Spanish means top or lid. The story is told that when a customer was served a drink, the barman covered the glass with a slice of bread to keep the flies out.

Competition among bars has always been keen, so to entice the customers elaborate titbits were offered. Some tapas can be picked up with the fingers but most are eaten with forks off little plates.

In Madrid there is the custom of chateo, a kind of 'pub crawl', seeking out the tavernas and bars where they serve the best tapas. Some tavernas offer as many as 40 to 50 different dishes. The places are crowded, especially before the midday meal or just before dinner, as people jostle for position at the bar where many of the tapas are displayed.

Spaniards enjoy snacks between meals, so the bars and tavernas are hardly ever empty. Some people will forego an evening meal as they spend their time chatting to friends, picking, nibbling and drinking sherry.

Despite their popularity, tapas are seldom served at home. I guess it would be hard to compete with chefs who all day long put their skills to the preparation of tapas.

While tapas are a kind of hors d'oeuvres, entremeses are hors d'oeuvres in the stricter sense of the word and home cooks serve them before a meal. The difference is not quite clear but the main distinction between entremeses and tapas is that the former are more elaborate and are served in larger quantities. To me, tapas and entremeses are great dishes to have before any meal, be it a modest family meal or a festive dinner party. One can always find the appropriate tapa or entremese to complement the rest of the meal.

Forn del Nastasi, Lérida, Catalonia

Forn del Nastasi is the type of restaurant that attracts local residents who come to eat local food. Always crowded, it serves the best food in town.

Lérida is of ancient origin. It was one of the battlefields of the Roman civil war on which Caesar defeated Pompey. The town has been built around a hill from which the citadel and cathedral dominate the landscape.

The province is part of Catalonia and in the north it extends into the high Pyrenees. Its rivers are rich in fish, especially trout which is very popular. In general, there is plenty of meat and game and they appear in hearty and tasty stews.

Right: The chef at Forn del Nastisi in Lérida presents some of the very tasty food he serves in his restaurant.
Left to right: Snails with a piquant butter; roasted legs of lamb; spicy sausages; grilled vegetables (p. 42) and black olives.

Migas a la Pastora

Shepherd's Crumbs

From El Cachirulo, Zaragoza, Aragón

Serves 6

750 g (1½ lb) fresh breadcrumbs
water
salt
125 g (4 oz) lard
4 cloves garlic, crushed

125 g (4 oz) button mushroom heads
125 g (4 oz) chorizo (spicy pork
    sausage), sliced
black olives for garnish

1. Sprinkle the breadcrumbs with water, just enough to moisten them, and with salt, cover with a damp cloth and refrigerate for 12 hours.
2. Melt and heat 100 g (3½ oz) of the lard, fry the garlic, add breadcrumbs and stir continuously over low heat for 10 minutes.
3. Fry the mushrooms and the chorizo slices.
4. Reserve 6 mushroom heads and chorizo slices for garnish, and mix the rest with the breadcrumbs.
5. Serve in an earthenware bowl garnished with mushrooms, chorizos and olives.

Chipirones a la Plancha

Baby Squid cooked on a Hotplate

From Restaurant Casa Costa, Barceloneta, Barcelona, Catalonia.

Serves 6

18 baby squid, cleaned
¼ cup (2 fl oz) olive oil
3 sprigs parsley, finely chopped
2 cloves garlic, crushed

1 tablespoon paprika
salt
freshly ground black pepper

1. Place the squid on a hotplate, or over charcoal, or into a heavy frying pan.
2. Sprinkle with oil and with half of a mixture of parsley, garlic, paprika, salt and pepper.
3. Keep sprinkling with oil, turn the squid after about 3 minutes, and sprinkle with the remaining mixture.
4. Cook for a further 3 minutes until brown.

Gambas a la Plancha

Prawns cooked on a Hotplate

From **Restaurant Casa Costa**, *Barceloneta, Barcelona, Catalonia.*

Serves 4

6 tablespoons olive oil
juice 2 lemons
1 clove garlic, crushed

salt
freshly ground black pepper
12 fresh king prawns, uncooked

1. In a screw-top jar, combine oil, lemon juice, garlic, salt and pepper. Shake well.
2. Pour the mixture into a bowl and add the prawns. Let them steep for a few minutes.
3. Place the prawns on a hotplate over an open charcoal fire or into a heavy-bottomed frying pan. Sprinkle with the mixture and cook the prawns on both sides for 4 to 8 minutes, depending on the size of the prawns. Serve hot and eat with fingers.

Albóndigas

Meatballs

Serves 6

375 g (12 oz) minced beef
125 g (4 oz) chorizo (spicy pork sausage), minced
½ teaspoon salt
freshly ground black pepper
1 clove garlic, crushed
2 sprigs parsley, finely chopped

1 teaspoon dried oregano
1 teaspoon paprika
2 eggs, lightly beaten
¼ cup (2 fl oz) brandy
4 tablespoons flour
½ cup (4 fl oz) olive oil

1. Combine all ingredients except flour and oil. Mix well and form the mixture into small balls.
2. Heat the oil in a heavy frying pan. Dip the meatballs in the flour and fry them in hot oil until brown. Serve hot on toothpicks.

SOUPS

When I think of Spanish soups, the first to come to mind is the Gazpacho – the light, refreshing, iced 'vegetable salad soup'. The maxim that the climate determines the style of food is exemplified in this creation of the heat of the Andalusian sun. It is of Moorish origin and the name is derived from the Arabic for 'soaked bread'.

Most Spanish soups are very much the result of what is locally available. They are rather heavy and in many instances are more like stews. When eaten with plenty of crusty fresh bread and washed down with lots of local wine, they are a nourishing meal in themselves. Along the coastline, fish and seafood soups contain whatever fish was in the nets of the morning's catch. It is interesting to note that soups from along the Mediterranean shores are related to the fish soups of other countries along its shores.

In the interior every region creates its own soups. So in Sevilla, in addition to the famous Gazpacho, there is the almond soup, while in Catalonia there is the Sopa de Galeta, a mixture of pork and pasta spiced with cinnamon and saffron. The Basque country is well known for its fresh green vegetables so it is not surprising to find green bean soup as typical of the region. Valencia has its rice soup. And in Galicia the Caldo Gallego combines white beans, chorizo, ham and bacon.

Nourishing soups made with dried beans, peas and lentils are very popular, and throughout the country the spicy chorizo sausage provides a typical 'Spanish flavour'.

El Burladero, Sevilla, Andalusia

Sevilla is among the most fascinating cities in Spain, a place of sun and shade, cool gardens, quaint narrow streets; of historical buildings and churches; the town of flamenco music, of festivals, famous bullfights, colourful people; and last, but not least, of good food.

Through the centuries it has attracted people who have come to experience the unique atmosphere of Sevilla and who have fallen under its spell. There is so much to see – Roman remains, the vestiges of Moorish times such as the Alcázar palace, the Giralda with its Christian superstructure, the cathedral, the third largest in Christendom, and innumerable churches and convents, palaces, Baroque civil buildings and gardens – all form a backdrop for the vibrant people of Sevilla. The town has never failed to inspire artists. It is the setting for such operas as Carmen and The Barber of Seville.

The sunny southern climate has greatly influenced the style of cooking of Andalusia in general and that of Sevilla in particular. Regional dishes are light and refreshing, and the people of Sevilla eat well but in moderation. The heat of the day which frequently persists into the night does not encourage heavy eating.

The famous Gazpacho, the chilled 'vegetable salad soup', is simple and refreshing. Tapas are popular, and the chefs of Sevilla are renowned for their skill in frying. Taverns specialising in morsels of seafood fried in a crisp batter are well patronised.

Sevilla is also well known for its bullfighting. It is with much pride that the restaurant El Burladero (which means 'refuge in a bullring') displays photographs of famous bullfighters. It also takes pride in serving typical regional dishes. On the menu, as well as a fine Gazpacho, are Huevos a la Flamenca, a tasty dish of eggs, vegetables and meat, and Cocido Andaluz, the local stew.

Right: Gaspacho (p. 16); oxtail with potatoes; and baked eggs with vegetables, ham and sausage (p. 38).

Gazpacho Andaluz

Iced Vegetable Salad Soup

From Restaurant El Burladero, Sevilla, Andalusia.
Most cooks in Spain have their own versions of Gazpacho; pine nuts may be used instead of almonds, and in some parts of the country finely diced meat or chicken is added. In Extremadura, game (especially rabbit meat) is used.
I have my own favourite Gazpacho, which I have prepared for years; and as it is quite different from the following recipe, I have included it below.

Serves 4-6

Soup:
3 tablespoons stale white breadcrumbs
1-2 cloves garlic, crushed, according to taste
1 tablespoon wine vinegar
1 tablespoon olive oil
1 green or red pepper (capsicum), seeded and chopped
1 onion, chopped
4 tomatoes, peeled and chopped
1 cucumber, peeled, seeded and chopped
8 almonds, finely crushed
iced water
salt
finely ground white pepper

Garnishes:
1 large cucumber, peeled, seeded and diced
1 green and 1 red pepper (capsicum), seeded and cut into small squares
2 tomatoes, peeled and cut into small dice
1 onion, finely chopped
2 hard-boiled eggs, chopped
2 slices stale white bread, cut into small dice

1. Combine all soup ingredients except the almonds, water, salt and pepper. Soak and refrigerate for 1 hour.
2. Purée in a blender or food processor.
3. Add almonds, salt, pepper and enough iced water to dilute to desired consistency.
4. Refrigerate for 3 to 4 hours before serving.
5. Arrange each of the garnishes in a separate dish, and place these in the centre of the table.
6. Serve the soup in chilled bowls. Each diner adds garnishes selected according to individual taste.

My Own Gazpacho

Serves 6

4 large tomatoes, peeled, seeded and
  diced
2 cucumbers, peeled, seeded and
  diced
1 green and 1 red pepper (capsicum),
  seeded and cut into small squares
½ onion, finely chopped
3-4 cups (24-32 fl oz) canned tomato
  juice

3 tablespoons olive oil
juice 1 lemon
1 clove garlic, crushed (optional)
salt
1 dash Tabasco sauce
3 sprigs parsley, chopped
12 black olives, stones removed

1. Combine all ingredients except parsley and olives. Use enough tomato juice to obtain desired consistency.
2. Refrigerate for 4 hours.
3. Serve in chilled bowls garnished with parsley and olives.

Sopa de Ajo Asturiana

Garlic Soup

Serves 6

½ cup (4 fl oz) oil
4-5 cloves garlic, finely chopped
250 g (8 oz) stale white bread, no
  crust, roughly crumbled
1 teaspoon paprika
salt

1 pinch cayenne pepper
4 cups (1 litre) water
3 ripe tomatoes, peeled and roughly
  chopped
2 eggs, lightly beaten
2 sprigs parsley, finely chopped

1. In a saucepan heat the oil, add garlic and sauté until garlic is soft but not brown.
2. Add the bread, and over moderate heat cook until light golden, but do not brown.
3. Add paprika, salt, cayenne, water and tomatoes. Simmer for 30 minutes over low heat.
4. With a wooden spoon beat the soup until bread disintegrates.
5. Keep beating, and add the eggs. Simmer for a few moments but do not boil.
6. The soup should be highly seasoned. If necessary, add more cayenne and salt. Garnish with parsley.

Caldo de Pescado

Galician Fish Soup

Serves 4-6

1 kg (2 lb) of two or three varieties of white-flesh fish (non oily), filleted
4 onions, chopped
2-3 cloves garlic, chopped
3 sprigs parsley, chopped
2 sprigs thyme, chopped
2 sprigs oregano, chopped
3 bay leaves

1 cup (8 fl oz) olive oil
1 tablespoon wine vinegar
5 cups (1.25 litres) water
1 cup (8 fl oz) dry white wine
salt
freshly ground black pepper
4-6 thick slices of toasted bread

1. Cut the fish fillets into 5 cm (2 in) pieces.
2. Make a marinade by mixing onions, garlic, parsley, thyme, oregano, bay leaves, oil and vinegar.
3. Place the fish pieces in a ceramic or glass bowl, and pour the marinade over them.
4. Refrigerate for 2 to 4 hours.
5. Transfer to a saucepan and add water, wine, salt and pepper.
6. Bring to the boil and simmer over low heat for 20 minutes.
7. To serve, place the bread into individual soup bowls and pour the hot soup over them.

Sopa de Cádiz

Fish and Rice Soup

Serves 4

1 large snapper head
4 cups (1 litre) water
salt
6 peppercorns
2 bay leaves
½ cup (3 oz) rice

2 tablespoons olive oil
1 onion, finely chopped
1-3 cloves garlic, according to taste
3 sprigs parsley, chopped
juice 1 lemon

1. Gently cook the fish head in the salty water, together with the peppercorns and bay leaves, for 30 minutes.
2. Take off the heat and allow to cool. Strain the stock and save all flesh from the fish head.
3. In the stock, cook the rice for 15 minutes.
4. In a frying pan, heat the oil and fry onion, garlic and parsley until onion is transparent.
5. Add the onion to the stock and cook for 10 minutes.
6. Add the flesh of the fish and lemon juice. Season to taste.
7. Serve hot with fresh crusty bread.

Right: The gardens, fountains and ancient buildings inside the Royal Alcazares, Seville.

Crema de Cangrejos

Cream of Crayfish Soup

From **Casa Duque**, *Segovia, Old Castile*

Serves 6-8

6 tablespoons oil
90 g (3 oz) butter
1 stalk celery, chopped
2 leeks, white part only, sliced
1 turnip, peeled and chopped
2 tomatoes, peeled and chopped
3 sprigs parsley, chopped
3 sprigs fresh herbs (oregano, thyme, majoram)
2 cloves
6 peppercorns

¼ cup (2 oz) rice
1 cup (8 fl oz) dry white wine
8 cups (2 litres) fish stock or water
500 g (1 lb) uncooked freshwater crayfish or prawns
¼ teaspoon Tabasco sauce (or ¼ teaspoon sliced hot peppers)
1 cup (8 fl oz) cream
salt
½ cup (4 fl oz) brandy

1. In a saucepan heat the oil and butter, add celery, leeks and turnip, and sauté until soft and lightly coloured.
2. Add tomatoes, parsley, the other herbs, cloves, peppercorns, rice, wine, and water or fish stock. Bring to the boil and simmer over low heat.
3. Place the crayfish or prawns on top, cover the saucepan and steam them for 10 minutes.
4. Set aside 6-8 of the crayfish or prawns (to be used as garnish later). Shell all the other crayfish or prawns and set the tails aside. Return the shells to the saucepan and mix them in.
5. Continue to simmer for 40 minutes.
6. Remove from heat, allow to cool, and purée in a food processor or rub through a sieve, or crush with a wooden spoon and rub through sieve.
7. Return the liquid to the saucepan, add Tabasco (or hot peppers), cream and seasoning. Add the crayfish or prawn tails, and heat but do not boil. If necessary add more stock, water or cream.
8. Heat the brandy, pour it into the saucepan, mix well.
9. Serve hot, each soup plate garnished with a whole crayfish or prawn.

Sopa de Lentejas Madrileña

Madrid Lentil Soup

Serves 6-8

2 onions, chopped
2 red or green peppers (capsicum)
3 tablespoons oil
750 g (1½ lb) brown lentils, unsoaked
6 tomatoes, peeled and chopped

3 carrots, sliced
1 teaspoon salt
freshly ground black pepper
2 bay leaves
6 cups (1.5 litres) water

1. Place the onions, the peppers (capsicum) and oil in a saucepan, cover and simmer over low heat until the onions are soft.
2. Add the rest of the ingredients and simmer over low heat for 2 hours.
3. The soup may be served either as-cooked or may be puréed in a blender or food processor. When processing remove the bay leaves.

Sopa Castellana

Castillian Soup with Ham, Chorizo and Eggs

*From **Casa Duque**, Segovia, Old Castile*

Serves 6

6 cups (1.5 litres) water or stock
1 ham bone
3 tablespoons olive oil
3 cloves garlic, crushed
6 bread slices
6 thick slices of Spanish ham or prosciutto

200 g (6½ oz) chorizo (spicy pork sausage), sliced
1 teaspoon paprika
salt
freshly ground black pepper
6 eggs

1. Preheat the oven to 230°C (450°F /Gas 8).
2. In a casserole, combine water or stock and ham bone. Simmer for 30 minutes.
3. In a saucepan, heat the oil, fry the garlic, add bread slices, ham and chorizo, and sauté until the bread browns lightly.
4. Add the paprika and cook for 2 to 3 minutes.
5. Add the ham bone stock, cook for 5 minutes, then season with salt and pepper.
6. Transfer to a ceramic bowl, break the eggs on top, and put the dish in the preheated oven for 2 to 3 minutes until the eggs set. Serve hot.

Sopa de Vainas

Basque Green Bean Soup

Serves 6

750 g (1½ lb) green beans, cut into
   1.5 cm (½ in) lengths
6 potatoes, peeled and cut into chunks
½ cup (4 fl oz) olive oil
3-4 cloves garlic

4-6 cups (1-1.5 litres) water
6 slices white bread
100 g (3½ oz) grated cheese
10 olives, stoned and cut into slices

1. Prepare the beans and potatoes just before cooking.
2. Heat 3 tablespoons of the oil and fry the garlic cloves until soft, but do not brown.
3. Crush the garlic in the oil.
4. Place the water in a saucepan, add crushed garlic with its oil, and the beans, potatoes and salt.
5. Boil for approximately ½ hour or until the potatoes break up.
6. Cut the bread slices in half and sprinkle them with the cheese.
7. To serve, place the bread in individual soup bowls and pour the soup over them. Serve garnished with olive slices.

Parador Nacional 'Via de la Plata' Merida
Paradors are Spanish government hotels situated throughout Spain. Some are newly built but many of them occupy old castles, convents, monasteries and palaces. One of the most attractive of the renovated and rebuilt old buildings is the one at Merida.

Some of the foundations date back to Roman days when Merida was Augusta Emerita, the town built by Emperor Augustus for the veterans of his legions. The Roman temple was converted into a basilica and later a convent was built there. The present structure is a Baroque building and during its life it has been a convent, a hospital, a gaol, and in 1929 it became a national tourist inn. Today its colonnaded courtyard provides welcome shade and the tall vaulted ceiling and thick convent walls of the halls and public rooms retain the cool night air.

The Parador is proud of its kitchen and features on the menu many regional dishes of Extremadura.

The white-washed exterior is full of simple charm and its Baroque belfries no longer feature bells but support huge stork nests from which the birds view the tranquil life of Merida.

Right: In the shady courtyard, on the edge of a well, rests a dish of baby lamb stew (p. 80).
Inset: The courtyard of the Parador Nacional Via de la Plata.

Sopa de Cantabria

Country Soup from Cantabria (Old Castile)

Serves 6-8

4 large potatoes, peeled and sliced
½ cup (4 fl oz) olive oil
4 tomatoes, peeled and cut into 1 cm
  (⅜ in) slices
4 onions, sliced

8 bread slices
3-4 cloves garlic, crushed
salt
8 cups (2 litres) water

1. Lightly sauté the sliced potatoes in 2 tablespoons of the oil. Set aside.
2. Lightly fry the tomato slices in 2 tablespoons of the oil. Set aside.
3. In a casserole, cover the bottom with some of the onion slices, then place 2 or 3 of the bread slices on top, then place a layer of some of the potatoes and then some of the tomatoes. Repeat until they are all used up.
4. Lightly fry the garlic in the rest of the oil and pour it on top.
5. Dissolve some salt in the water and pour it into the casserole, enough to cover the layers.
6. Bring it to the boil and simmer over low heat for 45 minutes. Serve hot directly from the casserole.

Sopa a la Valenciana

Valencian Rice Soup

Serves 6

6 cups (1.5 litres) water or meat stock
150 g (5 oz) chorizo (spicy pork
  sausage), sliced
2 sprigs oregano, chopped
2 sprigs thyme, chopped
3 sprigs parsley, chopped
2 bay leaves

6 peppercorns
3 tablespoons oil
2 onions, finely chopped
100 g (3½ oz) serrano ham
  (or prosciutto) cut into small cubes
3½ cups (21 oz) rice

1. Put the water or stock into a large saucepan, add the chorizo, oregano, thyme, parsley, bay leaves and peppercorns. Cook over medium heat for 35 minutes.
2. In another saucepan heat the oil, add the onions and fry until light golden.
3. Add the ham and the rice. Cook until the rice starts to colour.
4. Add the ham-sausage-rice mixture to the stock. Cover the saucepan and cook over low heat for 20 minutes.
5. Turn off the heat and let it stand for 10 minutes before serving.

Caldo Gallego

White Bean, Cabbage and Potato Soup

Serves 6

250 g (8 oz) dried white beans
6-10 cups (1.5-2.5 litres) water
2 chorizo (spicy pork sausage)
1 ham bone or smoked pork ribs
250 g (8 oz) Spanish ham or prosciutto
   cut into 1.5 cm (½ in) cubes
500 g (1 lb) potatoes, peeled and
   chopped

500 g (1 lb) cabbage or turnip tops,
   roughly chopped
1 onion, roughly chopped
salt
pepper
1 teaspoon paprika

1. Soak the beans overnight. Or boil 6 cups (1.5 litres) of water, add the beans and boil them for 2 minutes. Remove the saucepan from the heat and leave the beans to soak for 1 hour.
2. Bring the beans to the boil again.
3. Add the whole sausages, the ham bone or pork ribs, and the cubes of ham. Simmer over low heat for 1 hour.
4. Add the potatoes, cabbage and onion, season with salt and pepper, cover the saucepan and simmer as slow as possible for at least 2 hours.
5. Add paprika and cook for another 10 minutes.
6. To serve, remove and discard the bone, serve sausages and meat on a side plate, and the soup separately.

SAUCES

Two famous sauces – perhaps better known by their French names, Sauce Espagnol and Mayonnaise – are of Spanish origin.

Salsa Española, a brown sauce, was adopted by French chefs during the 19th century. It has become the basis of some of their famous sauces.

Cardinal Richelieu's visit in 1756 to Mahón on the island of Minorca is credited with the origin of the now world-famous mayonnaise. It is a direct descendent of the still popular ali-oli, the garlic-oil emulsion of Catalonian origin, used extensively on fish and vegetable dishes, as well as with some meats, especially when they are barbecued.

In Spain sauces are almost always an integral part of meat, fish and vegetable dishes and very few are served separately; so the flavour and character of the sauce is determined by the dish itself.

Restaurant Arzac, San Sebastián, Basque Provinces
Arzac has the reputation of being one of the best restaurants in Spain.

Juan Arzac is a friend and admirer of Michel Guérard and has been strongly influenced by the light style of Nouvelle Cuisine. He has created his own original and ingenious approach which is a combination of Nouvelle Cuisine, local methods and traditional ingredients.

Around San Sebastián, local specialities are mainly what the sea yields in a rich and varied harvest. Every day fresh seafood and fish are transformed under Arzac's creative direction into some of the best dishes I have eaten in Spain.

Chipirones en su Tinta, stuffed squid in a black sauce made from its ink, is a startling dish yet its flavour is unsurpassed.

Right: Clockwise from bottom: stuffed baby squid in its ink; fish pâté (p. 65); baked crab (p. 68); hake with seaweed.

Salsa Española

Spanish Sauce (*classic version*)

This is the most famous of Spanish sauces. It was adopted by the French cuisine and in France became the basis of many now-famous classic sauces.

60 g (2 oz) butter
1 onion, finely chopped
1 celery stalk, chopped
1 carrot, chopped
1 clove garlic, whole but peeled
3 tablespoons flour
2 bay leaves

6 peppercorns
100 g (3½ oz) minced beef
6 cups (1.5 litres) beef stock
  (see p. 141)
1 sprig each of thyme, parsley and
  oregano, tied together
salt

1. Melt the butter and sauté the onion, celery, carrot and garlic until the onion browns.
2. Add the flour and brown lightly.
3. Add bay leaves, peppercorns, meat, stock and herbs, bring to the boil, then simmer over low heat for 2 hours.
4. Strain and cook for a further 2 hours, skimming off spume which gathers on top. If it gets too thick, add more beef stock.
5. Season, and use as a sauce or as the basis for other sauces.

Salsa Española

Spanish Sauce (*simple version*)

60 g (2 oz) butter
2 onions, chopped
1 carrot, chopped
1 celery stalk, chopped
60 g (2 oz) ham or bacon, chopped

2 tablespoons flour
2 cups (16 fl oz) hot beef stock
  (see p. 141)
freshly ground black pepper
salt

1. In a saucepan melt the butter and fry the onions, carrot, celery and ham or bacon, until the vegetables are brown.
2. Stir in the flour and fry until flour colours.
3. Slowly stir in the stock, season, and simmer for 15 minutes.
4. Strain and use as a sauce or as the basis for other sauces.

Mayonesa

Mayonnaise

Makes 2 cups

3 egg yolks
1 tablespoon French mustard
2 cups (16 fl oz) olive oil

juice 1 lemon
salt
freshly ground black pepper

1. Place the egg yolks and mustard into a bowl and beat with a wire whisk until well blended.
2. Add the oil, drop by drop at first, then in a thin stream as the mayonnaise thickens.
3. Add the lemon juice, salt and pepper.

Ali-oli

Garlic Mayonnaise

A pestle and mortar, a mixer, a rotary hand beater or a food processor may be used. Originally a speciality of Catalonia.

Makes 2 cups (16 fl oz)

4-5 cloves garlic, crushed
2 egg yolks
1½ cups (12 fl oz) olive oil
½ teaspoon salt

pinch of cayenne pepper
juice 1 lemon
water

1. Mash garlic to smooth paste.
2. Add egg yolks and beat or process until they are thick and pale yellow.
3. While continuing to beat, gradually and slowly add the oil until all is used.
4. Season with salt and cayenne pepper, and stir in the lemon juice.
5. Stir in enough cold water to achieve desired consistency. Serve in separate bowl, with boiled, grilled or barbecued fish, meat or vegetables.

Salsa de Alcaparrado

Caper Sauce

60 g (2 oz) butter
2 tablespoons flour
1 cup (8 fl oz) hot beef stock
  (see p. 141)
2 tablespoons vinegar

½ cup (2 oz) capers, chopped
salt
freshly ground black pepper

1. Melt the butter, add the flour and cook until flour starts to colour.
2. While stirring, gradually add the hot stock and the vinegar. Cook for 10 minutes until sauce is smooth.
3. Add capers, salt and pepper. Serve with fish or with smoked meats.

La Picada Catalana

The Picada is not really a sauce in the true sense. It is used to flavour soups, stews, meat and fish dishes – added half-way through the cooking. There are regional variations, and different ingredients are used, but this is the basic recipe.
A food processor may be used instead of the traditional mortar.

¼ teaspoon saffron
2 cloves garlic, peeled
¼-½ teaspoon salt
30 g (1 oz) toasted, blanched almonds

30 g (1 oz) toasted, blanched hazelnuts
½ teaspoon cinnamon
2 sprigs parsley, chopped
¼ cup (2 fl oz) dry sherry

1. In a mortar, grind all dry ingredients to a fine paste.
2. Gradually add enough sherry to dilute to the desired consistency.

Sobrino de Botin, Madrid, New Castile
The area round the Plaza Mayor, the 'Main Square' of the old town of Madrid, is a warren of tiny streets branching off at all angles. For hundreds of years this was the centre of the busy town life. Shops, workshops, inns and hostelries provided and satisfied all the necessities of everyday life.

Here, in the street of the Cuchilleros, the Cutlers, towards the end of the 16th century, a licence was granted for the regal sum of 150 ducats, giving permission to the owners to take in paying 'living-in' guests. This was the beginning of the Sobrino de Botin as a hostel and naturally, as food was also served, the start of a tradition which has continued without interruption until the present. The hostel is long gone and the rooms on the first floor are now used as a restaurant. However the oven which was built in 1725 and used for roasting the now-famous Castilian roast meats, is still in use today.

The Botin is a very popular and busy place, and every week hundreds of suckling piglets and baby lamb not larger than a large serving platter are roasted in this oven.

The menu shows typical local dishes and the atmosphere of the place is characteristic of local eateries, which for many centuries have served local tradesmen and shopkeepers as well as having provided welcome rest and sustenance for the weary traveller.

Right: The kitchen at the Sobrino de Botin in Madrid, where meats, especially suckling pig, are roasted in the traditional wood fired oven.

Salsa Barbacoa Catalana

Catalán Barbecue Sauce

Traditionally this sauce is made with pestle and mortar. However, it may be easily prepared in a food processor.

Serves 4-6

4 cloves garlic
2 sprigs mint
12 toasted almonds
12 toasted hazelnuts
5 ripe tomatoes, peeled, seeded and
   chopped

salt
freshly ground black pepper
1 teaspoon vinegar
½ cup (4 fl oz) olive oil

1. In a mortar, crush garlic, mint and the nuts to a fine paste. Add tomatoes, salt, pepper and vinegar and continue until all ingredients combine to form a smooth sauce.
2. While stirring constantly, slowly (as for mayonnaise) pour in the oil. Serve with barbecued meats, fish or vegetables.

Romescu

Catalán Pepper Sauce

5 tomatoes
3 cloves garlic, whole but peeled
12 toasted almonds
12 toasted hazelnuts
½-1 teaspoon cayenne pepper,
   according to hotness desired

salt
1 cup (8 fl oz) olive oil
2 tablespoons vinegar
¼ cup (2 fl oz) sherry
1 sprig parsley, finely chopped

1. Heat the oven to 180°C (350°F/Gas 4).
2. Bake the tomatoes and garlic for 20 minutes. Cool, peel the tomatoes and remove their seeds.
3. In a mortar or food processor, make a paste with the nuts. Add tomatoes, garlic and salt, and continue until the mixture has a smooth texture.
4. Slowly and gradually add the oil, thoroughly incorporating it into the sauce before adding more. It should be thick and creamy.
5. Finally add vinegar and enough sherry to achieve desired consistency. Stir in the parsley.
6. Refrigerate overnight to allow flavours to blend. Serve with grilled or boiled meats, fish or other seafood.

Salsa de Piñones

Pine nut Sauce

From **Restaurant Forn del Nastasi** *Lérida, Catalonia.*

Serves 4

½ teaspoon cumin seeds, crushed
100 g (3½ oz) pine nuts
1 clove garlic
2 hard-boiled egg yolks

2 cups (16 fl oz) chicken stock
 (see p. 140)
salt
freshly ground black pepper

1. In a mortar or food processor, make a fine paste from the cumin, pine nuts, garlic and egg yolks.
2. Gradually add the stock, season, and put it in a saucepan. Bring to the boil and simmer over low heat for 15 minutes. Serve with barbecued or roasted chicken.

EGG DISHES

Eggs are used extensively in Spanish cooking and appear in many dishes. At the beginning of the meal they are used in soups – in the simple Sopa de Ajo, the peasant garlic soup, they are either poached on top or stirred into the soup. When hard boiled, they are sliced or chopped and used for garnish.

They form part of many of the greater variety of tapas, the delicious hors d'oeuvres. Eggs Flamenca are a tasty and very typical way of presenting eggs; here they are cooked over a layer of sofrito (the thick sauce-like mixture of vegetables and ham) and attractively garnished with fresh green peas, asparagus tips and green and red pimentos.

The most famous and popular of all egg dishes is the Tortilla, the Spanish omelette. Basically a dish of sautéed potatoes, onions and eggs, it appears in all parts of Spain and there must be as many varieties of it as there are cooks in Spain. In Extremadura hot peppers are used in the Tortilla, while in Barcelona macaroni is added. In Madrid they use kidneys, and in Granada lambs' brains give the dish a delicate flavour.

Eggs also play an important part in the preparation of Spanish desserts and sweets.

Huevos a la Riojana

Scrambled Eggs with Tomatoes and Chorizo

Serves 4

6 tomatoes, peeled, seeds removed
  and chopped
30 g (1 oz) lard
6 eggs, well beaten
salt
freshly ground black pepper

2 sprigs parsley, finely chopped
6 slices bread, cut into triangles
¼ cup (2 fl oz) olive oil
100 g (3½ oz) chorizo (spicy pork
  sausage), cut into slices

1. Fry the tomatoes in the lard until they thicken.
2. Add the eggs, season, add parsley and scramble the eggs.
3. Separately fry the bread triangles in the oil until brown; also fry the chorizo.
4. Add bread and chorizo to the eggs, and serve hot.

Restaurant 'El Candil', Salamanca, León

Salamanca boasts two cathedrals and three universities. One of the schools was founded in 1218 and is the oldest in Spain.

It is an impressive town, especially if you approach it crossing the river over the Roman bridge. The distinctive outline of the cathedrals dominates the hillside that rises from the river.

A student of architecture and Spanish language will be well rewarded here, as the town is a treasure of ancient buildings and its libraries house some of the most valuable books and manuscripts in Spain.

The town has a lot of local colour. Student and townfolk mingle in the Plaza Mayor where on festive days processions and bands delight the crowds. There are many coffee houses, inns and restaurants, some of them enjoying well-deserved reputations.

El Candil serves simple, hearty local food, spicy hams and sausages, egg dishes such as the Huevos a la Charra, and some good wines from La Ribera.

Right: Clockwise from bottom left: Spanish cured ham, spicy sausage; fried eggs with an assortment of sausage and grilled pork chop.

Tortilla con Espárragos

Omelette with Asparagus

Restaurant Sobrino de Botin, Madrid, New Castile.

Serves 1

3 asparagus spears
2 eggs
salt

freshly ground black pepper
2 tablespoons water
15 g (½ oz) butter

1. Cut the asparagus spears into 2.5 cm (1 in) lengths, put the pieces into boiling salted water for 3 minutes, then drain them.
2. In a bowl, beat the eggs with salt, pepper and water.
3. In a small frying pan, heat the butter, pour in the egg mixture and add the asparagus.
4. Cook until the mixture sets. To serve, fold in half and serve hot.

Tortilla

Spanish Potato and Onion Omelette

There are many variations of this basic recipe. Fried chorizo, chopped ham or cooked chicken meat, or cooked vegetables such as chopped red or green pepper (capsicum), beans, spinach, peas or asparagus pieces may be added to the onions and potatoes or, if desired, can replace them.

Serves 4

1 cup (8 fl oz) olive oil (no substitutes)
2-3 potatoes, peeled and sliced or cut
  into small cubes
2 large onions, chopped

salt
freshly ground black pepper
4 eggs

1. Heat the oil in a medium-sized frying pan, add the potatoes and onions, and season. Cover with a lid and sauté over low heat, stirring from time to time, for 15 to 20 minutes.
2. Whip the eggs in a large bowl until frothy.
3. When the potatoes and onions are tender, remove them from the frying pan and put them into the egg mixture. Mix well together.
4. Drain off most of the oil from the frying pan, leaving just enough to cover the bottom of the pan.
5. Reheat the oil and pour in the egg-vegetable mixture. With a fork, distribute the vegetables evenly and flatten the top. Fry over low heat.
6. When the mixture has set, cover the frying pan with a plate and invert the tortilla on to it. Then slide the tortilla back into the pan and continue frying until it is done. Alternatively you may place the tortilla under a preheated grill to finish off the top.
7. The tortilla should look like a firm cake. It may be eaten hot or cold and is very tasty with a green salad.

Tortilla Estilo Badajoz

Hot Pepper Omelette

*From **Parador Nacional 'Via de la Prata'**, Mérida, Extremadura*

On my way to Badajoz, which is on the Portuguese border, I came across local farmers turning the red peppers spread out to dry on huge canvas sheets in the warm late autumn sun. The colours were magnificent.

Serves 4

200 g (6½ oz) chorizo (spicy pork sausage), sliced
3-4 tablespoons olive oil
1 small thin hot red or green pepper, seeded, washed and sliced

1 teaspoon paprika
8 eggs
2 tablespoons water
salt

1. In a frying pan, sauté the sausage in 2 tablespoons of oil.
2. Add the peppers and paprika, lightly sauté over low heat for 10 minutes.
3. In a bowl, whip the eggs well with water and salt.
4. If necessary, add more oil to the frying pan, then pour in the eggs, stir with a fork and fry until set.
5. Fold it over, divide into 4, and serve to those who like it hot!

Huevos de Toledo

Fried Eggs with Ham, Peas and Mushrooms

*From **Hostal del Cardenal**, Toledo, New Castile*

Serves 6

100 g (3½ oz) butter
250 g (8 oz) Spanish ham or prosciutto, chopped
6 mushrooms, finely chopped
250 g (8 oz) cooked green peas
6 eggs

salt
freshly ground black pepper
1 red pepper (capsicum), seeded and cut into strips
12 olives, pitted

1. In a frying pan, heat half of the butter and sauté the ham and mushrooms until mushrooms start to brown. Add peas. Then remove from the pan, set aside and keep warm.
2. Melt the rest of the butter and fry the eggs.
3. To serve, place the ham mixture on preheated plates, put the egg on top, then garnish with red pepper strips and olives.

Huevos a la Flamenca

Baked Eggs with Vegetables, Ham and Sausage

*From **Restaurant El Burladero**, Sevilla, Andalusia*

Serves 4

1 cup (8 fl oz) olive oil

2 potatoes, peeled and cut into small dice

1 onion, chopped

1 clove garlic, crushed

1 red or green pepper (capsicum), seeded and chopped

2 slices serrano ham, prosciutto or lean smoked ham, chopped

1 chorizo (spicy pork sausage), sliced

200 g (6½ oz) green peas, cooked

200 g (6½ oz) green beans, cooked, cut into small pieces

1 small can asparagus tips (use fresh asparagus, when in season)

4 tomatoes, peeled, juice and seeds squeezed out, chopped

2 tablespoons tomato paste

½-1 cup (4-8 fl oz) water

salt

freshly ground black pepper

4 eggs

an additional ½ red or green pepper (capsicum), seeded and cut into strips

6 small sprigs parsley for garnish

1. Preheat the oven to 200°C (400°F /Gas 6).
2. Heat the oil in a large frying pan and fry potatoes until golden. Remove, and set them aside.
3. In the same pan, fry onion, garlic, chopped pepper, ham and chorizo (but keep 6 slices for garnish) until the onions are soft and transparent.
4. Add peas (keep some for garnish), beans, asparagus tips (keep some for garnish), tomatoes, tomato paste, the potatoes and water. Season, and cook over low heat until most of the liquid has evaporated. Stir occasionally.
5. Use either a large ovenproof dish or 4 individual dishes (in Spain glazed earthenware dishes are used). Brush the inside with oil and pour in the vegetable mixture.
6. Make four hollows and break the eggs into them.
7. Garnish the top with slices of chorizo, peas, asparagus tips and strips of red or green pepper.
8. Bake in the preheated oven for 15 to 20 minutes until the egg whites turn opaque.
9. Serve decorated with sprigs of parsley.

Right: A formal garden nestles between the Parador Raimundo de Borgoña and the mediaeval walls of Ávila.

Pisto Castellano

Egg Scrambled with Vegetables

*From **Mesón de Rastro**, Ávila, Old Castile*

Serves 4

2 tablespoons olive oil
2 onions, chopped
60 g (2 oz) bacon, chopped
4 potatoes, peeled and cut into small
   dice
2 zucchini (courgettes), sliced
4 tomatoes, peeled and chopped

3 red or green peppers (capsicums),
   seeded and chopped
1½ cups (12 fl oz) meat stock
4 eggs
salt
freshly ground black pepper
triangles of fried bread made from
   4 slices

1. Heat the oil in a large frying pan, and sauté the onion and bacon.
2. Add the potatoes and zucchini, cover, and cook for 5 minutes.
3. Add tomatoes, peppers and stock. Simmer over low heat until liquid is reduced by half.
4. Whip the eggs with salt and pepper, and add to the mixture. Cook until eggs are set. Stir occasionally.
5. Serve with the fried bread.

Tortilla a la Magra

Omelette with Roast Pork

*From **Hostal del Cardenal**, Toledo, New Castile*

Serves 4

¼ cup (2 fl oz) olive oil
500 g (1 lb) potatoes, peeled and
   sliced
salt
freshly ground black pepper

8 eggs, well beaten
100 g (3½ oz) Spanish ham or
   prosciutto, chopped
4 slices roast pork

1. In a frying pan, heat the oil and sauté the potatoes. Season.
2. Add the ham to the beaten eggs and pour the mixture over the potatoes.
3. Fry the omelette until done on one side.
4. Using a plate, invert the pan so that the omelette lays on the plate. Slide the omelette (uncooked-side down) back into the pan.
5. Place the pork slices on top, complete the cooking and serve hot.

Tortilla al Sacromonte

Omelette with Lamb Brains

From **Restaurant Sevilla**, *Granada, Andalusia*

Serves 4

¼ cup (2 fl oz) olive oil
100 g (3½ oz) minced lamb
1 lamb's brain, finely chopped
100 g (3½ oz) Spanish ham or
   prosciutto, finely chopped
30 g (1 oz) fresh peas
1 red or green pepper (capsicum),
   seeded and finely chopped

8 eggs, beaten
salt
freshly ground black pepper
1 artichoke heart (tinned)
1 teaspoon tomato purée
4 long slices of chorizo (spicy pork
   sausage)

1. Heat the oil and sauté the meat, brains, ham, peas and the pepper until the meat is cooked.
2. Add the eggs and seasoning. Fry first on one side, then turn the pan upside down on to a plate and slide the tortilla (uncooked side down) back into the pan and fry until cooked.
3. Garnish, and serve hot or cold. To garnish, fill the centre of the artichoke heart with tomato purée and place it in the centre of the tortilla, then place 4 long slices of chorizo radiating from the centre.

Tortilla Madrileña con Riñones

Omelette with Kidneys

From **Sobrino de Botin**, *Madrid, New Castile*

Serves 4

4 tablespoons olive oil
90 g (3 oz) butter
2 onions, chopped
3 lambs' kidneys, chopped
3 sprigs parsley, finely chopped
½ cup (4 fl oz) dry sherry

salt
freshly ground black pepper
4 tomatoes, cut in half
125 g (4 oz) Spanish ham
6 eggs, well beaten

1. Heat half of the oil and butter in a frying pan, and sauté 1 chopped onion until soft and transparent. Add kidneys and parsley and cook for 5 minutes.
2. Add the sherry, bring to boiling point and season with salt and pepper. Remove the mixture from the pan, set aside and keep it warm.
3. Heat the rest of the oil and butter and fry the tomatoes. Remove them from pan, set aside and keep them warm.
4. In the same pan, sauté the remaining onion, add the ham, pour in the eggs, and season. Fry on both sides.
5. Serve the omelette on a heated serving plate, with the kidney heaped in the centre, surrounded by the tomatoes.

VEGETABLES AND SALADS

The people of Spain share in what seems a Mediterranean tradition of eating vegetables as a separate course. If one looks for reason, one may find it in the fact that many 'main course' dishes, especially the stews, contain a large proportion of vegetable and it seems redundant to serve more vegetables alongside.

Regardless of reasons, there is a wide variety of excellent vegetables in Spain. From the cooler and wetter climate of the north, through the dry central plateaus, to the hot weather of the south, every possible vegetable is grown. In addition, the Canary Islands and the Spanish islands in the Mediterranean supply a wide range of subtropical varieties.

Beans, peas and lentils form an important part of the cuisine, especially in winter, when dried they find their way into nourishing stews – many of which are all vegetable. In a country where meat has never been plentiful, the pulses are a considerable source of protein.

In Spain you find that vegetable dishes are usually a composition of a number of types of vegetable eaten as a separate course, or as the main course, or frequently as the whole meal served with thick slices of crusty, fresh bread.

Escalibades

Grilled Vegetables

From **Forn del Nastasi**, *Lérida, Catalonia*
Traditionally the vegetables are grilled over an open fire but a hot grill may be used.

Serves 4-6

4 red peppers (capsicums), cut in half and seeded
4 small eggplant (aubergine), whole
4 tomatoes, whole
4 onions, whole
1 cup (8 fl oz) olive oil

1 sprig parsley, finely chopped
1 clove garlic, crushed
salt
freshly ground black pepper

1. Preheat the griller and place the vegetables under. Turn them, keep grilling until they are blackened all round. Allow to cool.
2. To make the dressing, combine oil, parsley, garlic, salt and pepper in a screw-top jar and shake well.
3. Peel the grilled vegetables, cut them into strips, pour the dressing over and serve them with grilled or roasted meats.
   This can also be served as a first course with an ali-oli sauce (see p. 29).

This can also be served as a first course with an ali-oli sauce (see p. 29).

Right: A proud display at the Forn del Nastasi of some of the fresh ingredients used in the preparation of the rich cuisine of inland Catalonia.

Ensalada Especial 'Sevilla'

Mixed Salad 'Sevilla'

From **Restaurant Sevilla**, *Granada, Andalusia*

Serves 4-6

1 tomato, peeled and cut into wedges
¼ of a small firm lettuce, chopped
6 fresh beans, thinly sliced
1 small carrot, grated
6 asparagus spears (canned)
2 artichoke hearts (canned), cut into pieces
2 pieces of heart of palm, sliced

½ small leek, white part only, thinly sliced
½ cup (4 fl oz) olive oil
2 tablespoons vinegar or lemon juice
salt
freshly ground black pepper
4 hard boiled eggs, peeled, cut into wedges

1. In a bowl, gently mix the vegetable ingredients.
2. Combine oil, vinegar or lemon juice, salt and pepper in a screw-top jar and shake well.
3. Pour the dressing over the salad and serve garnished with the egg wedges.

Jamón con Habas

Broad Beans with Ham

From **Restaurant Sevilla**, *Granada, Andalusia*

Serves 6

1 kg (2 lb) fresh broad beans
salt
30 g (1 oz) lard

200 g (6½ oz) Spanish ham or prosciutto, chopped

1. Simmer the broad beans in salted water for 15 minutes until they are cooked. Cool.
2. Peel the beans, fry them in lard for 10 minutes over low heat. Add ham and cook for a further 5 minutes. Serve hot.

Pisto Manchego

Vegetable Stew

From **Hostal de Cardenal**, *Toledo, New Castile*

Serves 4

4 tablespoons olive oil
60 g (2 oz) bacon, chopped
2 onions, chopped
4 zucchini (courgettes), diced

2 red or green peppers (capsicums), seeded and chopped
4 tomatoes, peeled, seeded and chopped
salt
freshly ground black pepper

1. Heat the oil, add the bacon and fry without browning for 2 to 3 minutes.
2. Add the onions and sauté until soft and transparent.
3. Add zucchini, peppers and tomatoes, season, and simmer over low heat until some of the liquid evaporates. If necessary skim off surplus fat. Serve as a vegetable with cooked or roasted meats.

Judías Verdas a la Española

Spanish Green Beans

From **Sobrino de Botín**, *Madrid, New Castile*

Serves 4

1 kg (2 lb) green French beans, sliced
salt
4 tablespoons olive oil
2 onions, chopped
3 cloves garlic, crushed
4 sprigs parsley, chopped
4 large tomatoes, peeled and chopped

salt
freshly ground black pepper
100 g (3½ oz) Spanish ham or prosciutto, cut into cubes
1 tablespoon vinegar
½ teaspoon crushed cumin seeds

1. Cook the beans in salted water for 10 minutes. Rinse with cold water, and set aside.
2. Heat half of the olive oil and sauté 1 chopped onion, 2 of the garlic cloves and half of the parsley until the onions are soft and transparent.
3. Add the tomatoes, season, and cook for 15 minutes. Rub through a sieve and set aside.
4. Heat the remaining oil and sauté the remaining onion and garlic and the ham, then add the vinegar, the reserved tomato sauce and the remaining parsley.
5. Bring to the boil, add the reserved beans and the cumin seeds, season to taste, and simmer for 15 minutes. Can be served as a separate vegetable course or with roast meat.

Espinacas a la Catalana

Spinach with Raisins, Pine Nuts and Anchovies

Serves 4

2 kg (4 lb) spinach
½ cup (4 fl oz) olive oil
1 clove garlic, crushed
4 fillets of anchovy, chopped

½ cup (2 oz) pine nuts
1 tablespoon raisins
salt
freshly ground black pepper

1. In a large saucepan, boil some water and cook the spinach for 3 minutes. Drain, and chop it roughly.
2. In a frying pan, heat the oil and lightly sauté the garlic, add anchovies, spinach, pine nuts and raisins, and season. Cook over low heat for 20 minutes. Serve as a separate course or with other dishes.

Ensalada Sevillana

Sevillian Salad

From **Restaurant El Burladero**, *Sevilla, Andalusia*

Serves 8

6 red or green peppers (capsicums),
    cut in half and seeded
4 cups (20 oz) cooked rice
4 onions, finely sliced
6 tomatoes, peeled and each cut into
    8 segments
200 g (6½ oz) green olives, may be
    pitted if preferred

½ cup (4 fl oz) olive oil
2 tablespoons vinegar
1 clove garlic, crushed
salt
freshly ground black pepper

1. Place the pepper halves (skin side up) under a preheated grill until the skin blackens. Cool and remove the skin. Cut the peppers into strips.
2. Put the rice on the bottom of a serving dish, and on top arrange the pepper strips, onions, tomatoes and olives.
3. In a screw-top jar, make a dressing from the oil, vinegar, garlic, salt and pepper. Shake well and pour over the salad.

Right: A wooden pavilion in the Viveros Gardens, Valencia which was used in lavish exhibitions around the turn of the century.

Cebollas Rellenas a la Catalana

Stuffed Onions

From **Restaurant Forn del Nastasi**, *Lérida, Catalonia*

Serves 4

8 large onions, peeled
½ cup (3 oz) rice
2 cups (16 fl oz) stock or water
2 cloves garlic, crushed
2 red or green peppers (capsicums),
  chopped
2 tablespoons olive oil

2 hard-boiled eggs, finely chopped
salt
freshly ground black pepper
½ cup (1 oz) fresh breadcrumbs
30 g (1 oz) butter softened

1. Preheat oven to 180°C (350°F /Gas 4).
2. Cut the top off each onion about one-third from the top end. Set the tops to one side.
3. In a saucepan, boil some water, add the onions and cook for 1 minute.
4. Take out the centre of each onion, leaving an outer casing of 2 or 3 layers. Set the centres aside.
5. Boil the rice in 1 cup of stock for 15 minutes.
6. Finely chop the tops and centres of the onions and, together with the garlic, add to the rice.
7. Sauté the chopped peppers in the oil for 15 minutes.
8. Add the peppers to the rice, then add the chopped eggs and season.
9. Stuff the onion casings, place them in a baking dish. Add the remaining stock, cover the dish and place in the preheated oven. Bake for 45 minutes.
10. Remove the cover, sprinkle the onions with breadcrumbs, turn the oven up to 200°C (400°F /Gas 6), and bake for a further 15 minutes until the breadcrumbs turn brown.

Maíz Español

Spanish Corn

Serves 4

2 tablespoons olive oil
corn stripped from 4 corn cobs, about
  2 cups
2 tablespoons flour
salt
cayenne pepper
¼-½ teaspoon chilli powder (optional)

1 cup (4 oz) grated Parmesan-style
  cheese
1 onion, finely chopped
12 olives, pitted and roughly chopped
1 clove garlic, crushed
4-6 tomatoes, peeled and finely
  chopped

1. Preheat the oven to 180°C (350°F /Gas 4).
2. In a saucepan, combine oil, corn, flour, salt, cayenne and chilli powder (optional) and cook over low heat for 10 minutes, stirring constantly.
3. Add cheese, onion, olives, garlic and tomatoes.
4. Pour it into a small casserole, and bake in the preheated oven for 30 to 40 minutes. Serve as a separate course.

Habas de Victoria

Broad Beans with Ham and Chorizo

Serves 4

broad beans from 2 kg of broad bean
  pods
150 g (5 oz) Spanish ham or
  prosciutto, in one piece

150 g (5 oz) bacon or speck, in one
  piece
200 g (6½ oz) chorizo (spicy pork
  sausage), in one piece
salt

1. Put the beans in a saucepan and cover with water, put the ham, bacon or speck and chorizo on top. Cover and simmer over low heat for 30 to 40 minutes.
2. Pour off the liquid and reserve for later use.
3. Cut the ham, bacon or speck and chorizo into small pieces.
4. Put the beans in a serving dish, season if necessary, put the meat on top of the beans, and serve as a separate course.

Espárragos Andaluz

Asparagus with Bread Sauce

*From **Restaurant Sevilla**, Granada, Andalusia*

Serves 4

½ cup (4 fl oz) olive oil
2 cloves garlic, chopped
1 slice white bread
500 g (1 lb) asparagus, cut into 1.5 cm
  (½ in) pieces
1 cup (8 fl oz) chicken stock
  (see p. 140)

salt
freshly ground black pepper
2 teaspoons white wine vinegar
8 triangles of fried bread (croûtons)

1. In a saucepan, heat the oil and lightly sauté the garlic. Remove, and reserve.
2. In the same oil, fry the slice of bread until crisp. Remove, and reserve.
3. In a saucepan, simmer the asparagus pieces in the stock over low heat for 12 minutes. Season and add vinegar.
4. In a mortar, crush the fried garlic and the bread and use a little of the stock to make a paste.
5. Add this to the asparagus, making sure it is not too liquid. Stir and cook for 3 minutes. Serve with the croûtons.

RICE DISHES

Rice, introduced by the Arabs, is one of the staples of Spain and few people in Europe are as experienced and skilfull in its preparation as the Spanish cooks. Today it is used extensively throughout the country, but nowhere is it transfigured into a greater variety of dishes than along the eastern shores of Spain.

Valencia is undoubtedly the rice capital of Spain. Here the best rice is grown. Mud-walled paddies called planteles are a typical sight, and not surprisingly the best rice dishes originate from this region.

Loving care goes into the cooking of rice. Centuries of experience have taught the chefs to judge the right amount of liquid, the balance of flavours arising out of the use of varying ingredients. The strong aromas of the sea combine with the flavours of poultry or meats. The subtle fragrance of saffron, herbs and spices give the rice dishes their unmistakably Spanish flavour.

The ultimate creation and best-known rice dish of Spain is the paella. Its opulent flavour and extravagant appearance have put the paella among the great dishes of the world. Yet, if you follow the time-honoured method of preparation, it is not a hard dish to cook. While it is best put together in a paellera – the shallow, round dish from which it derives its name – a large, shallow frying pan will do the trick. There are many versions of the paella and any combination of fish and seafood available on the day, together with any type of meat, poultry or game, can be used. Oil, rice and saffron are the only constant ingredients.

Between the paella, the greatest of rice dishes, and the Arroz con Azafrán, the simple saffron rice, the Spanish cooks created a whole range of dishes worth trying.

Restaurant Viveros, Valencia, Valencia

Valencia has been called the city of eternal Spring. Sparkling clear light, bright blue skies, this is the background of one of Spain's most attractive cities. People here love to celebrate, and frequent festivals throughout the year enliven religious and civic occasions.

The winding narrow streets, churches, historical buildings, squares and gardens give the town a character of its own. The cathedral is a good example of the changes that have taken place through the ages: the three portals, Romanesque, Gothic and Baroque, represent the three main styles that flourished in Valencia.

The town has always been rich – its prosperity derived from the irrigated fertile alluvial plain, the Huerta, where rice is cultivated. It is therefore understandable that many regional dishes include rice and that the paella should be its crowning glory. The people of Valencia insist that theirs is the only genuine preparation. Indeed, it is difficult to argue; the one I tried was full of the subtle aroma of the shellfish and had the rich texture of saffron rice.

Valencia has always been an important commercial and fishing port and it is from here that many inland places, especially Madrid, are supplied with the best of Mediterranean seafood.

In Valencia one can always eat well, and with two and sometimes three harvests a year most vegetables are never out of season.

The Viveros Restaurant is set against the background of the Royal Gardens. It is a modern place but it serves some of the best regional food in Valencia. Typical dishes such as Arroz de Langosta (roasted lobster), Lubina 'Llobarro' Albufera (a local fish stew) and Fideua (seafood noodles) regularly appear on the menu.

Right: Clockwise from bottom left: Richly decorated seafood noodles (p. 68); lobster with rice (p. 57); fish stew with potatoes (p. 62) and the Albufera fish stew (p. 62).

Paella a la Valenciana

There are many types of paella which vary according to the produce available locally. Meat, chicken, even game, together with vegetables and spicy sausages, are used in the interior; while along the coast around Valencia a combination of seafood, meat, chicken and rice is preferred. Further north in Barcelona, only fish and shellfish are popular. There are no strict rules, and whatever seafood and meat is available goes in to the paellera. The addition of sherry will greatly improve the taste.

Serves 6-8

3 tablespoons olive oil
2 cloves garlic, crushed
2 onions, chopped
2 red peppers (capsicums), seeded and cut into strips
1 small chicken, cut into small pieces
250 g (8 oz) pork, ham or beef, diced
4 tomatoes, peeled and quartered
750 g (1½ lb) rice
4-6 cups (1-1.5 litres) chicken stock (see p. 140), enough to cover
¼ teaspoon saffron

125 g (4 oz) shelled peas
125 g (4 oz) fresh kidney beans
6 artichoke hearts (optional)
500 g (1 lb) cod, whiting or hake, cut into small pieces
1 crayfish, cut into small pieces
250 g (8 oz) raw prawns, shelled and de-veined
3 sprigs parsley, chopped
salt
freshly ground black pepper

1. Heat the oil in a paellera or large frying pan, add the garlic, onions, pepper strips, chicken pieces and meat. Sauté until the meat browns.
2. Add the tomatoes, stir in the rice and cook over low heat for 5 minutes.
3. Add the stock, saffron, peas, beans and artichoke hearts (optional). Cook for 10 minutes.
4. Add the fish and prawns, cook gently for 10 to 15 minutes, adding more stock if necessary. The rice should be moist but not soggy.
5. To serve, take out some of the meat, fish, prawns, peas and capsicums and arrange them in a decorative pattern on top. Sprinkle with parsley, and set the paellera or pan on the table.

Arroz con Vino de Jerez

Rice with Sherry

Serves 4

2 tablespoons oil
1 onion, chopped
1¼ cups (8 oz) short grain rice
1 cup (8 fl oz) sweet sherry

1½-2 cups (12-16 fl oz) chicken stock (see p. 140)
30 g (1 oz) butter
salt
freshly ground black pepper

1. Heat the oil in a saucepan, and sauté the onion until soft and transparent.
2. Add the rice and, while stirring, cook for 2 minutes.
3. Add the sherry, cook, and when it has been absorbed add enough stock to cover the rice.
4. Cover the saucepan and over a low heat cook for 20 minutes.
5. Before serving, add butter and season to taste.

Paella Alicantina

The combination of rabbit (or chicken) with mussels and prawns is unusual and delectable. This simple paella is worth trying.

Serves 4-6

3 tablespoons olive oil

salt

freshly ground black pepper

1 rabbit or chicken, cut into small pieces

1 clove garlic, bruised

400 g (13 oz) short grain rice

4 cups (1 litre) salted boiling water in which 2 pinches saffron have been boiled

24 fresh mussels

8-12 fresh uncooked prawns, shelled and de-veined

2 red peppers (capsicums), seeded and cut into strips

1. Heat the oil in a paellera or large frying pan. Season the meat and fry until brown but not completely cooked. Remove the meat and keep it warm.
2. Fry the garlic long enough to flavour the oil. Discard the garlic.
3. Lower the heat, add the rice to the pan, and cook for 2 to 3 minutes.
4. Turn up the heat and add the boiling saffron water, enough to cover the rice.
5. Cover the pan and cook over low heat for 20 minutes.
6. Add the meat and place the mussels and prawns on top. Decorate with the strips of red pepper.
7. Cover the pan, cook for a few minutes until the mussels open and the prawns are cooked. Serve directly from the pan.

Paella Catalana

Catalan Paella

*From **Casa Costa**, Barceloneta, Barcelona, Catalonia*

Serves 4-6

1 cup (8 fl oz) olive oil
2 cloves garlic, peeled
1 onion, finely chopped
one 1.5 kg (3 lb) chicken, cut into
  pieces
2 tomatoes, peeled and finely chopped
an additional 1 clove garlic, crushed
4 cups (1 litre) chicken stock
  (see p. 140)
2 cups (13 oz) rice
250 g (8 oz) fresh peas
10 green beans, cut into 2 cm (¾ in)
  pieces

2 artichokes, trimmed, tough leaves
  and choke removed, cut into
  quarters
¼ teaspoon cayenne pepper
salt
½ teaspoon saffron
250 g (8 oz) white fish fillets, cut into
  pieces
6-8 prawns, shelled and de-veined
12 mussels, scrubbed
24 pipis or clams

1. In a paellera or large frying pan, heat the oil, add the 2 whole cloves of garlic and fry them until they are brown. Remove and discard the garlic.
2. Add the onion and chicken pieces and fry to brown them.
3. Add tomatoes, crushed garlic and chicken stock, and bring slowly to the boil.
4. Gradually add rice, spreading it evenly over the surface.
5. Add the peas, beans, artichokes, cayenne pepper, salt, saffron and boil fast for 5 minutes.
6. Lower the heat, add the fish, prawns, mussels and pipis, and cook over low heat without stirring until the rice has absorbed all the liquid, for about 20 minutes. The rice should be light but fairly dry. Serve directly from the paellera.

Hostal del Cardenal, Toledo, New Castile

It's been suggested that if you have only one day in Spain, spend it seeing Toledo.

The Imperial City of Toledo is indeed a unique, fascinating place which has witnessed two thousand years of history.

It occupies an impressive position in the Castilian plain, and its picturesque setting has been an inspiration to many poets and artists, among them El Greco, who captured the dramatic feeling of violent and sharp light, angry clouds, and the stark flatness of the surrounding arid countryside.

The town is quite small and a walk through the winding streets reveals at every turn some new and unexpected vista. The whole place is a living museum of architectural styles spanning many centuries and cultures, as for hundreds of years it was the centre of Arab, Jewish and Christian co-existence. It would be interesting to go back over the ages and follow the various culinary styles that accompanied the diverse people who held power over Toledo. Today the food is mainly that of Old Castile and particularly of La Mancha, the country of Cervantes and Don Quixote.

The Hostal del Cardenal is tucked away in a peaceful garden setting behind the city walls, next to the Gate of Alfonso VI. Once part of the residence of a cardinal, it offers local food such as Partridge Toledo Style and Tortilla a la Magra.

Right: *Interior of Hostal del Cardenal.*

Arroz a la Marinera

Rice with Fish, Mussels and Prawns

Serves 4-6

½ cup (4 fl oz) olive oil
1 onion, finely chopped
750 g (1½ lb) white-fleshed fish fillets
  (250 g of each of three varieties),
  cut into 5 cm (2 in) pieces
1 tablespoon paprika
2 sprigs thyme, chopped
2 cups (13 oz) short grain rice

4-5 cups (1-1.25 litres) fish stock
  (see p. 140)
2 cloves garlic, crushed
½ teaspoon saffron
salt
12-18 mussels, cleaned
12 fresh prawns, uncooked

1. In a paellera or large frying pan, heat the oil, sauté the onions and brown the pieces of fish.
2. Add the paprika, thyme and rice, spreading it evenly in the dish. Cook for 2 to 3 minutes.
3. Add the stock (about twice the volume of rice), and bring it to the boil.
4. Stir in garlic, saffron and salt.
5. Place the mussels and the prawns on top of the rice and cook over medium heat for 15 minutes or until all liquid is absorbed. Serve directly from the pan.

Mejillones con Arroz

Mussels with Rice

Serves 4

48 mussels
1 clove garlic, crushed
2 sprigs parsley, chopped
½ cup (4 fl oz) dry white wine
2 cups (16 fl oz) water
2 tablespoons oil
2 onions, chopped

400 g (13 oz) short grain rice
salt
freshly ground black pepper
¼ teaspoon saffron
1 red pepper (capsicum), seeded and
  cut into strips

1. Place the mussels in a large saucepan, add garlic, parsley, wine and water. Bring to the boil and cook only until mussels open. Take off the heat, strain, save the liquid, and take the mussels out of the shells and put aside.
2. Heat the oil in a saucepan and fry the onions until soft and transparent.
3. Stir in the rice and cook for a few minutes.
4. Add enough of the mussel liquid to cover rice; if there is not enough, add water. Season and bring to the boil.
5. Add saffron and pepper strips, cover the pan and cook over low heat for 20 minutes.
6. Take off the heat, add mussels, and let it stand for 10 minutes before serving.

Arroz de Langosta

Lobster with Rice

From **Restaurant Viveros**, *Valencia*

Serves 6

1 cup (8 fl oz) oil
3 lobsters each 500 g (1 lb), cut
  lengthwise and de-veined
salt
2 tomatoes, peeled and chopped

2 cloves garlic, crushed
1 teaspoon paprika
4 cups (1 litre) fish stock (see p. 140)
½ teaspoon saffron
2 cups (13 oz) rice

1. In a paellera 50 cm (20 in) in diameter, or large frying pan, heat the oil, add lobster halves and brown them. Add salt, tomatoes and garlic, stir and simmer for 2 to 3 minutes.
2. Add paprika and stock, bring to the boil, add saffron and rice, stir.
3. Arrange the lobster halves on top of the rice and cook over high heat.
4. Turn down heat and cook without stirring for 20 minutes. Serve from dish.
   In the original recipe the dish is placed in a medium oven for the last 6 minutes.

Arroz a la Murciana

Rice with Pork, Tomatoes and Peppers

Serves 4-6

½ cup (4 fl oz) olive oil
1 kg (2 lb) lean port shoulder, cut into
  2.5 cm (1 in) cubes
2 cloves garlic, peeled
500 g (1 lb) ripe tomatoes, peeled and
  chopped
6 red or green peppers (capsicums),
  seeded and cut into strips

½ teaspoon saffron
4 sprigs parsley, finely chopped
5 cups (1.25 litres) water
2 cups (13 oz) short grain rice
salt
freshly ground black pepper

1. Preheat the oven to 180°C (350°F/Gas 4).
2. Heat the oil in a heavy-lidded casserole and brown the pork. Remove it and set aside.
3. In the oil, brown the whole garlic cloves, remove and set aside.
4. Add the tomatoes and pepper strips to the oil and cook over low heat.
5. In a mortar or food processor, crush the fried garlic cloves together with the saffron and parsley.
6. Return the pork and garlic-parsley mixture to the casserole. Add 1 cup (8 fl oz) water, cover and cook over medium heat for 20 minutes.
7. Stir in the rice and cook for 2 to 3 minutes. Add 4 cups (1 litre) water, sufficient to cover the rice. Season.
8. Cover the casserole and place it in the preheated oven for 30 minutes until the meat is tender. Serve with a piquant green salad.

FISH

It is not surprising that a large part of the reputation of the Spanish cuisine is based on its fish dishes. Some 2500 kilometres of coastline washed by the waters of the Atlantic and the Mediterranean have bred a hardy race of fishermen who daily bring in a rich and varied harvest from the sea.

However, what is surprising is the fact that good and fresh seafood is readily available in virtually any part of inland Spain. Spaniards are so proud of their fish that they have worked out an efficient and speedy way of getting the precious, perishable cargo to most country centres.

The visitor to Madrid soon realizes why the city has such a high reputation for seafood. Spanish housewives are critical buyers. Fish and other seafood have to pass a thorough examination for freshness and quality before they finish up in the shopping basket.

Naturally enough, the best quality and selection of fish is to be found along the coast. Many cities, towns and regions with direct access to the sea compete for the reputation of being the best. To me, they are all good. The main thing is they are all different. Just compare the Catalan Zarzuela de Mariscos, that shellfish stew of many flavours especially when eaten in Barcelona, with the greatest of rice dishes, the paella of Valencia, which is also an exceptional seafood dish. They certainly are among the best in Western cooking.

In the south you will find more exotic combinations, grouper in sherry sauce, tuna cooked with olives, and of course swordfish grilled over charcoal embers.

In the north, the Basques claim that they are the best chefs in Spain. They certainly have a wide variety of fish from.the cold waters of the Atlantic. Undoubtedly the fresh sardines I have eaten in Santander, an important fishing port on the Bay of Biscay, were delicious.

Galicia, in the north-west, supplies the country's major share of seafood. The local scallop, its shell the symbol of St James, the patron saint of Spain, is among the best in the world. The cool waters of the Atlantic yield every conceivable type of fish, so it is not surprising that many Spanish fish dishes originate in this region.

Restaurant Casa Costa, Barceloneta, Barcelona, Catalonia

Barcelona is without doubt the most fascinating city in Spain, bursting with vitality and a joy of life which demonstrates itself in a cosmopolitan lifestyle. Among its many attributes is the high standard of cuisine. You can eat the food of many countries, but what is most important is that it is the centre of the best of Catalán regional cooking.

Throughout the ages Barcelona's life and well-being has been linked to the sea. Today, as in the past, it is Spain's most important port so it is not surprising that most of the local specialities are made from seafood.

Rice is the basis of many dishes, and it was here that I ate my best paella. I was lucky to taste the three most typical of local dishes at the same meal. The paella was followed by Zarzuela, a mixture of baked fish of the day with prawns, lobster, squid and mussels, colourful and delicious. Then, as though I had not had enough seafood, a Parrillada, grilled mixed fish. All of this was washed down with a refreshing chilled Tarragona white.

Casa Costa is one of many popular seafood eating places along the foreshore of Barceloneta, the colourful sailors' quarters. The restaurant, a huge timber shack overlooking the beach, was packed when I was there and long queues formed as eager diners waited to partake in a seafood feast.

Right: Clockwise from bottom left: mixed grilled seafood, famous Zarzuela (p. 64) and Paella (p. 54).

Truchas Gran Duque

Trout with Ham

*From **Casa Duque**, Segovia, Old Castile*

Serves 6

Sauce:
½ cup (4 fl oz) olive oil
2-3 cloves garlic, crushed
200 g (6½ oz) Spanish ham or
   prosciutto, finely chopped
3 sprigs parsley, finely chopped
2 bay leaves
salt
freshly ground black pepper

6 plate-size trout
¼ cup (1 oz) flour
½ cup (4 fl oz) oil
6 slices Spanish ham or prosciutto

1. Preheat the oven to 200°C (400°F /Gas 6).
2. To make the sauce, heat the oil in a saucepan and sauté the garlic.
3. Add chopped ham, parsley and bay leaves, and sauté until the ham is crisp. Season.
4. Dust the trout with flour, heat the oil in a frying pan and sauté the trout.
5. Place the trout in a shallow ovenproof dish, place the ham slices on top of the trout, pour the sauce over, and bake in the preheated oven for 10 minutes. Serve hot, directly from the oven dish.

Merluza a la Gallega

Hake with Potatoes and Peas

*From **Anexo Vilas**, Santiago de Compostela, Galicia*

Serves 6

1 kg (2 lb) potatoes, peeled
1 onion, quartered
2 cloves garlic
2 sprigs parsley, chopped
salt
6 steaks of hake or any white-fleshed
   fish, each 250 g (8 oz)

100 g (3½ oz) peas
½ cup (4 fl oz) oil
1 tablespoon paprika
freshly ground black pepper

1. In a saucepan, boil in water the potatoes, onions, 1 clove of garlic, parsley and salt for 15 minutes.
2. Reduce heat, and add the fish and peas, and simmer for 10 minutes.
3. In a frying pan, heat the oil and sauté the remaining garlic clove for 5 minutes, then remove it. Add paprika and sauté for 3 minutes. Season.
4. Drain the water from the fish and slice the potatoes.
5. On the bottom of an earthenware casserole, arrange the potato slices, then the fish, and sprinkle the peas on top. Pour the oil and paprika over this, and serve hot.

Besugo Asado

Baked Bream

From **Casa Duque**, *Segovia, Old Castile*

Serves 8

500 g (1 lb) potatoes, peeled and
  sliced
2 onions, sliced
3 cloves garlic, crushed
2 bay leaves
¾ cup (6 fl oz) oil
2 bream, each 1 kg (2 lb)
salt
2 tablespoons flour

16 small tomatoes
3 sprigs parsley, finely chopped
an additional 1 clove garlic, crushed
1 cup (8 fl oz) dry white wine
juice 2 lemons
salt
freshly ground black pepper
½ cup (2 oz) breadcrumbs

1. Preheat the oven to 200°C (400°F/Gas 6).
2. Cover the bottom of a shallow fireproof dish with a layer of potatoes, onions, garlic and bay leaf. Sprinkle with 3 tablespoons oil.
3. Place over low heat and sauté for 30 minutes.
4. Make 3 incisions in the flesh of each fish. Sprinkle them with salt and flour.
5. Place the fish in the dish and sprinkle with two tablespoons oil.
6. Arrange whole small tomatoes around the fish.
7. To make the sauce, heat 2 tablespoons of oil in a saucepan, sauté the garlic and parsley, add wine and lemon juice, season and pour over the fish.
8. Mix the breadcrumbs with the remaining oil, and sprinkle over the fish.
9. Bake in preheated oven for 30 to 45 minutes until fish is cooked.

Truchas en Escabeche

Pickled Trout

From **Hostería Nacional 'Del Comendador**, *Cáceres, Extremadura*

Serves 6

6 small trout
½ cup (2 oz) flour
½ cup (4 fl oz) olive oil

Marinade:
1 onion, finely chopped
3 carrots, sliced

3 bay leaves
3 cloves garlic, crushed
1 teaspoon paprika
3 cups (24 fl oz) dry white wine
2 cups (16 fl oz) vinegar
salt

1. Sprinkle the trout with flour and fry them in oil until they are cooked.
2. To prepare the marinade, combine all ingredients in a saucepan.
3. Bring the marinade to the boil and cook for 10 minutes.
4. Place the trout in a dish deep enough to contain the marinade. Pour the hot marinade over the fish, cool and refrigerate for at least 12 hours before serving. The marinade may be reused. Serve the trout on a plate, with a vegetable salad.

Lubina 'Llobarro' Albufera

Albufera Fish Stew

From **Restaurant Viveros**, *Valencia*

Serves 4

⅓ cup (2 fl oz) olive oil
12 blanched almonds, crushed
2 cloves garlic, crushed
2 sprigs parsley, chopped
1 teaspoon paprika
2 teaspoons flour
4 cups (1 litre) fish stock (see p. 140)

1.5 kg (3 lb) fillet of white-fleshed fish, cut into pieces
1 small hot chilli, chopped
salt
100 g (3½ oz) fresh shelled peas
strips of cooked red pepper (capsicum) for garnish

1. Heat the oil in a casserole. Sauté the almonds, garlic and parsley until the almonds lightly change colour.
2. Add paprika and flour, stir well and cook for 2 to 3 minutes without browning the flour.
3. Mix in the fish stock and, while stirring, cook until the sauce thickens.
4. Add fish pieces and chilli, season, and cook for 5 minutes.
5. Add peas and cook for a further 5 minutes or until the peas are cooked. Decorate with cooked strips of red pepper (capsicum) and serve from the dish.

'Nougat' de Rape

Fish Stew with Potatoes

From **Restaurant Viveros**, *Valencia*

Serves 6

½ cup (4 fl oz) oil
1.5 kg (3 lb) potatoes, peeled and cut into quarters
1-2 hot chilli, seeded and chopped (according to taste)
50 g (1½ oz) pine nuts
2 cloves garlic

4 dried red peppers (capsicums), chopped
2 tomatoes, peeled and chopped
1 kg (2 lb) eel or white-fleshed fish, cut into pieces
4 cups (1 litre) water
salt

1. Heat oil in a casserole. Sauté potatoes and chilli until potatoes brown but are not fully cooked.
2. In a mortar or food processor, grind pine nuts, garlic, red peppers (capsicums) and tomatoes.
3. Add to the potatoes and simmer for a few minutes.
4. Add the fish and half the water, simmer for 10 minutes. Add rest of water, season and cook for 5 to 10 minutes until it thickens slightly. Serve hot from the dish.

Right: View of cathedral in Salamanca.

Zarzuela de Pescado

Mixed Fish Dish

From **Casa Costa**, *Barceloneta, Barcelona, Catalonia*

This is a very popular Catalan dish. The ingredients vary according to what is available from the day's catch. It should include at least two types of white fish, prawns, lobster, mussels or squid.

Serves 4

500 g (1 lb) of white fish (buy 250 g (8 oz) each of two types such as bream, snapper, jewfish or whiting), cut into pieces

½ cup (2 oz) flour

4 tablespoons olive oil

2 cloves garlic, crushed

3 tomatoes, peeled and chopped

2 sprigs parsley, chopped

½ cup (4 fl oz) dry white wine

¼ cup (2 fl oz) brandy

1 tablespoon paprika

¼ teaspoon saffron

6 blanched almonds, crushed

salt

freshly ground black pepper

1 cup (8 fl oz) fish stock (see p. 140)

1 lobster, de-veined and cut into pieces

12 prawns, uncooked

12 mussels, scrubbed

1. Preheat the oven to 230°C (450°F/Gas 8).
2. Dust the fish pieces with flour, heat the oil in a large pan and brown the fish. Set them aside.
3. In the same oil, sauté the garlic, tomatoes and parsley.
4. Add white wine, brandy, paprika, saffron, crushed almonds, salt and pepper and the fish stock. Cook for 10 minutes.
5. Add the fish, stir gently and cook for 5 minutes.
6. Add the lobster pieces, prawns and mussels, cook for about 5 minutes.
7. Place the dish in the preheated oven. To serve, arrange the lobster pieces, prawns and mussels in a decorative pattern on top and serve without delay.

Esqueixada de 'Bacalla'

Cod with Olives and Tomatoes

From **Forn del Nastasi**, *Lérida, Catalonia*

Serves 4

¾ cup (6 fl oz) olive oil

2 onions, finely chopped

4 tomatoes, peeled and chopped

salt

400 g (13 oz) dried and salted cod, soaked overnight and rinsed

100 g (3½ oz) black olives, pitted

1. Heat the oil in a casserole, brown the onions, add tomatoes, season, and cook for 15 minutes.
2. Add cod, simmer for 10 minutes, remove from heat and let it stand for 1 hour.
3. Add olives, and refrigerate for 2 to 3 hours before serving.

Pâté de Cabracho

Fish Pâté

From the **Gran Casino del Sardinero***, Santander, Old Castile*

Makes 1 large pâté mould

1.5 kg (3 lb) fish fillets
8 eggs
1 cup (8 fl oz) cream, chilled
½ cup (4 fl oz) port wine
2 tablespoons whisky
2 tablespoons brandy
salt
white pepper
60 g (2 oz) fresh peas
1 red or green pepper (capsicum),
 finely chopped
1 clove garlic, crushed
10 asparagus spears, cooked

Sauce:
2 cups (16 fl oz) mayonnaise
 (see p. 29)
2 tablespoons whisky
1 teaspoon mustard
1 tablespoon dry sherry
1 tablespoon black caviar or fish roe
1 tablespoon red caviar or fish roe

1. Preheat the oven to 180°C (350°F/Gas 4).
2. Lightly poach the fish fillets in some water.
3. Break up the pieces and put them in a large bowl to cool.
4. With a wooden spoon, beat in the eggs one by one. Make sure they are well incorporated with the fish.
5. Continue beating and gradually incorporate the cream, port, whisky and brandy. Season.
6. Gently mix in the peas, chopped pepper and garlic.
7. In a greased pâté mould, place a layer of the mixture 2.5 cm (1 in) deep.
8. Arrange some of the asparagus spears so they do not touch each other. Place another layer of the fish paste, then more asparagus, and repeat until all is used up, with a layer of fish paste on top.
9. Cover the mould with aluminium foil, place the mould in a baking dish almost filled with hot water. Put it in the preheated oven and cook for 1½ hours or until the pâté has set.
10. To make the sauce, mix the sauce ingredients together.
11. Cool the pâté, remove from mould. Cut the pâté into slices, mask with the sauce, and serve with slices of toast.

Fideos con Almejas

Noodles with Clams

From **Anexo Vilas**, *Santiago de Compostela, Galicia*

Serves 6

½ cup (4 fl oz) oil
1 clove garlic, crushed
2 onions, chopped
2 red or green peppers (capsicums),
    seeded and roughly chopped
2 tomatoes, peeled and chopped
2 sprigs parsley, chopped

1 kg (2 lb) clams or pipis
2 cups (16 fl oz) water
300 g (10 oz) spaghetti-type noodles
¼ teaspoon saffron
salt
freshly ground black pepper

Heat the oil in a saucepan and sauté garlic, onions, peppers, tomatoes and parsley until onions are soft and transparent.

2. Place the clams in a separate saucepan, add water and heat until clams open.
3. Drain the water into the saucepan with the onion mixture. Bring this to the boil, add noodles and cook until they are done to your liking.
4. Add the clams and saffon, and season to taste. Serve hot with fresh crusty bread.

Anexo Vilas, Santiago de Compostela, Galicia

The shrine of St James the Apostle is one of the most important places of worship in the whole of Christendom, and Santiago de Compostela is the third holy city, after Rome and Jerusalem. Since the 9th century, when the reputed burial place of St James was discovered, countless pilgrims have journeyed there from all over the world.

It is a wealthy town, richly decorated in the extravagant manner of the Baroque. The cathedral is the focal point; originally Romanesque in style, its elaborate facades and opulently carved towers dominate their surroundings.

Throughout the year there are many festivities but none so rich in colour as St James's Day, 25 July. Celebrations start on the night before, with magnificent fireworks – the 'Fuego del Apóstol' – and continue with religious services, colourful processions and, of course, lots of good food.

The region of Galicia is most famous for its seafood which the waters of the Atlantic provide. Needless to say, it is fish and other seafood that is eaten on most feast-days. There is the famous livestock fair on Ascension Day, 20 May, when large quantities of octopus are eaten. It is therefore not surprising that many of the specialities served at Anexo Vilas are of the sea. Most of them are hearty stews that originated in the kitchens of the fishing families. The famous Pulpo con Patatas is a rich octopus stew; and equally well known is Merluza a la Gallega, hake with herbs, potatoes and peas.

The food in Santiago is not all fish. The fertile countryside provides good meat, especially pork. Lacón con Grelos, a combination of white beans, fresh or pickled hand of pork, with cabbage and turnip tops, is rich and delicious when prepared by the Anexo Vilas. Local wines are robust and go well with the flavoursome Galician fare.

Right: Moncho Vilas with some of the local specialities. Clockwise from bottom left: octopus with potatoes; hake with potatoes and peas (p. 60); noodles with clams (p. 66); tart of St James (p. 92) Vieira pie.

Changurro al Horno

Baked Crab

*From **Restaurant Arzac**, San Sebastián, Basque Provinces*

Serves 4

4 crabs
green parts of 2 leeks
3 sprigs parsley, chopped
4 onions, finely chopped
¼ cup (2 fl oz) olive oil
white parts only of 2 leeks, finely chopped
2 carrots, finely chopped

1 clove garlic, crushed
1 tablespoon tomato paste
1 cup (8 fl oz) brandy
salt
freshly ground black pepper
60 g (2 oz) butter, softened
½ cup (2 oz) breadcrumbs

1. Cook the crabs in salted water with the green part of the leeks, parsley and 2 of the chopped onions for 10 minutes. Cool in the water. Reserve the stock.
2. Open the crab and take out the meat. Set the meat aside. Reserve the shells (for serving).
3. In a frying pan, heat the oil and sauté the remaining chopped onions, the white part of the leeks, the carrots and garlic, until onions are soft and transparent.
4. Add tomato paste and the broken-up crab meat.
5. Heat the brandy and pour it flaming into the mixture.
6. Pour in some crab stock to moisten the mixture, cook over low heat for 5 minutes. Season.
7. Fill the shells. Mix the butter and breadcrumbs, and sprinkle over the top.
8. Place under a preheated griller and leave long enough to brown the top. Serve in the shells.

Fideua

Seafood Noodles

*From **Restaurant Viveros**, Valencia*

Serves 6-8

½ cup (4 fl oz) olive oil
500 g (1 lb) small lobsters, cut into pieces
500 g (1 lb) prawns, shelled but tails left on, and de-veined
300 g (9½ oz) eel or white-fleshed fish
2 cloves garlic, crushed
2 tomatoes, peeled and chopped

1 teaspoon paprika
4 cups (1 litre) fish stock (see p. 140) or water
¼ teaspoon saffron
salt
1 kg (2 lb) thick noodles

1. In a paellera or large frying pan 50 cm (20 in) in diameter, heat the oil and lightly sauté lobster, prawns, eel and garlic.
2. Add tomatoes, paprika, fish stock, saffron and salt.
3. Bring to the boil, add noodles and simmer over low heat. The dish should be neither runny nor too dry. Serve from the dish.

Chipirones en su Tinta

Stuffed Baby Squid in its Ink

From **Restaurant Arzac**, *San Sebastián, Basque Provinces*

Serves 4

32 small squid
½ cup (4 fl oz) olive oil
2½ onions, finely chopped
1 clove garlic, crushed
salt
freshly ground black pepper
2 red or green peppers (capsicums),
   seeded and chopped

2 tomatoes, peeled, seeded and
   chopped
1 clove garlic, whole, unpeeled
1 slice white bread without crust
2 cups (16 fl oz) fish stock (see p. 140)
12 triangular croûtons

1. Clean the squid, reserve the ink, and chop the tentacles finely.
2. In a pan, heat half of the oil and sauté 2 of the chopped onions, the garlic and the chopped tentacles until the onions are soft and transparent. Season to taste.
3. Remove the ingredients but leave the oil in the pan for later use.
4. Mix the tentacles and onion well. With a teaspoon, place a little of the onion-tentacle mixture into each squid, making sure that it is not filled too firmly. Secure the opening with a toothpick.
5. To make the sauce, add the rest of the oil to the pan, heat it and sauté the chopped half onion, peppers, tomatoes, 1 whole unpeeled garlic clove and the bread.
6. Add the fish stock mixed with the ink, and cook over low heat for 2 to 3 minutes.
7. Rub the sauce through a fine sieve, or purée it in a processor and then rub through a sieve.
8. Return the sauce to the pan, season and cook for a few minutes.
9. Gently add the squid and simmer until sauce has thickened. Serve with small triangular croûtons.

Sardinas con Tomate

Sardines with Tomatoes

From **Forn del Nastasi**, *Lérida, Catalonia*

Serves 4

⅓ cup (2 fl oz) olive oil
8-12 fresh sardines (depending on
   size), cleaned
3 tablespoons flour
salt

freshly ground black pepper
2 cloves garlic, crushed
1 kg (2 lb) tomatoes, peeled and
   chopped
2 sprigs parsley, chopped

1. Heat the oil in a pan, sprinkle the sardines with flour, season with salt and pepper, and fry briefly. Take out of the oil and set aside.
2. In the same oil, sauté the garlic, add tomatoes and simmer for 10 minutes.
3. Add sardines and simmer over low heat for 5 minutes. Season to taste, and serve sprinkled with parsley.

POULTRY AND GAME

Spanish cooks put a great deal of flavour into anything they prepare and nowhere does it come into the fore more aptly than in the preparation of poultry dishes, especially chicken.

Although, as in most countries, battery-bred chickens are sold in the shops, you can still buy a fresh plump old-fashioned farmyard chicken. If you really care for the old traditions, a live pollo from the local market will be very rewarding – as long as you can put up with the mess.

In Andalusia they cook chicken in a sherry sauce. In Aragon the obvious preparation will be in Chilindrón Sauce; it is here that this sauce is at home and used also with lamb, rabbit or pork. In the Basque Country chicken will be served with tomatoes and with local mountain ham, which incidentally is frequently used in chicken dishes throughout the country. I guess it is to add the flavour that poultry often lacks.

Duckling with olives is a typical Spanish way of serving this bird and it is particularly tasty when, as in Andalusia, sherry or Madeira is also used in the cooking.

I did not come across any goose dishes, and I presume the dry climate of the Iberian Peninsula is not very conducive to the breeding of this bird.

Gamebirds are eaten throughout the country. In Toledo pheasant is a local speciality. Partridge is a great delicacy, usually cooked with lots of fresh herbs, bacon or pickled pork and sometimes with cabbage as in the Andalusian dish Perdices con Col. Quail is best when simply grilled over a charcoal fire and served sprinkled with herbs and lemon juice.

In the past hunting game was the privilege of the nobles but today the fields resound with the sharp sound of shots as the autumn season starts.

El Cachirulo, Zaragoza, Aragón

El Cachirulo is a most interesting complex of restaurants. It calls itself 'the regional monument of gastronomy'. Built in the style of an Aragonese country villa, it has numerous dining rooms, a cellar and the typical local bar. Here hams and tasty sausages hang from the beams, while on the bar counter are tapas to tempt the drinkers.

The waiters are dressed in traditional costume and in the evening, the jota, a combination of dance and song, is performed.

I was there in October on the eve of the festival of Our Lady of El Pilar. El Cachirulo was crowded with people eager to taste the wide variety of Aragonese specialities for which the restaurant is justifiably famous.

Right: Clockwise from bottom right: Shepherd's Crumbs (p. 12); cod with garlic; eggs in sauce with asparagus tips; peaches in wine (p. 93); roast baron of lamb (p. 80); chicken in chilindron sauce (p. 72).
Inset: Interior of El Cachirulo.

Pollo en Chilindrón

Chicken in Chilindrón Sauce

*From **El Cachirulo**, Zaragoza, Aragon*

Serves 4-6

½ cup (4 fl oz) olive oil
1 clove garlic, chopped
1.5 kg (3 lb) chicken, cut into pieces
salt
freshly ground black pepper
1 onion, chopped
2 red or green peppers (capsicums),
  seeded and chopped

1 tablespoon paprika
¼ teaspoon saffron
200 g (6½ oz) Spanish ham or
  prosciutto, cut into cubes
250 g (8 oz) tomatoes, peeled and
  chopped
½ small hot pepper, seeded and
  chopped

1. Heat the oil in a casserole and sauté the garlic. Remove it when it is cooked.
2. Add the chicken pieces, season, and brown on all sides. Remove the chicken and set aside.
3. Sauté the onion and peppers (capsicums) until they are soft. Add paprika, saffron, ham and tomatoes.
4. Mix the browned chicken pieces and the hot peppers into the sauce, cover and simmer it over low heat for about 1 hour or until the chicken is tender. To serve, arrange the chicken pieces on a platter and cover with sauce.

Pollo Extremeño

Chicken in Red Wine

*From **Parador Nacional 'Via de la Plata'**, Mérida, Extremadura*

Serves 4

¼ cup (2 fl oz) olive oil
1.5 kg (3 lb) chicken, cut into 8 pieces
salt
1 cup (8 fl oz) strong beef stock
  (see p. 141) [a beef cube may be
  used to boost the flavour]

½ cup (4 fl oz) dry red wine
45 g (1½ oz) butter
fried bread sippets (croûtons)

1. Heat the oil in a casserole and brown the chicken pieces on all sides. Season.
2. Add stock and wine, bring to the boil.
3. Add butter, cover, and simmer over low heat for 1 to 1¼ hours until chicken is tender. Serve hot in soup bowls, garnished with the sippets.

Olla Podrida

Chicken Stew with Chickpeas

One of the many versions of the Olla Podrida

Serves 6

2 cups (12 oz) chickpeas, soaked
  overnight
4 slices of bacon, cut into 4 cm (1½ in)
  pieces
8 cups (2 litres) water
1.5 kg (3 lb) chicken, cut into pieces

125 g (4 oz) chorizo (spicy pork
  sausage), sliced
1 clove garlic, crushed
1 tablespoon paprika
salt

1. In a saucepan combine chickpeas, bacon and water, bring to the boil, cover and simmer over low heat for 2 hours.
2. Add the rest of ingredients and simmer for a further hour or until the chicken is tender.

Pepitoria de Gallina

Chicken Stew with Peas, Mushrooms and Olives

Serves 4

1.5 (3 lb) chicken, cut into pieces
salt
freshly ground black pepper
½ cup (2 oz) flour
¼ cup (2 fl oz) olive oil
2 onions, chopped
5 tomatoes, peeled and chopped
1 teaspoon sugar

1 red or green pepper (capsicum),
  seeded and chopped
water
1 cup green peas
125 g (4 oz) small button mushrooms
1 cup chopped and stoned green or
  black olives
flour and water for thickening

1. Sprinkle the chicken with salt, ground pepper and half of the flour.
2. Heat the oil in a casserole and brown the chicken pieces. Remove, and set aside.
3. In the same oil, sauté the onions, add tomatoes, sugar, some salt and the chopped pepper, then simmer over low heat for 10 minutes.
4. Add chicken pieces and enough water to cover them. Cover the casserole and simmer for 1 hour.
5. Add peas, mushrooms, olives and enough flour mixed with a little water to thicken the sauce. Simmer for 15 minutes, check seasoning and serve hot.

Pato con Aceitunas

Andalusian Duckling with Olives

Serves 4

2 tablespoons olive oil
45 g (1½ oz) butter
3 onions, sliced
2 carrots, sliced
1.5 kg (3 lb) duckling
1 tablespoon flour
1 cup (8 fl oz) stock, hot

salt
freshly ground black pepper
1 cup (8 fl oz) Madeira or dry sherry
3 tablespoons tomato paste
2 sprigs parsley, finely chopped
48 green olives, pitted

1. Use a large heavy pan with lid or casserole deep enough to accommodate the duckling. Heat the oil and butter in the pan, add onions, carrots and duckling and fry over medium heat until the duckling is light golden brown. Remove duckling and vegetables and keep them warm.
2. Stir the flour into the fat, cook for 2 to 3 minutes and, while stirring constantly, add the hot stock. Season.
3. Add wine, tomato paste and parsley and cook for 5 minutes, stirring constantly.
4. Put duckling and vegetables back into the pan, cover, and simmer over low heat for 1¼ hours until duckling is tender.
5. Put the duckling on a serving plate, remove excess fat from sauce, strain into a saucepan, add olives, check the seasoning, and simmer only long enough to heat the olives. To serve, pour the sauce over the duckling.

'Las Pocholas', Hostal del Rey Noble, Pamplona, Navarre

The best restaurant in Pamplona, Las Pocholas, is run by six sisters. Here a variety of local Navarrese food is served.

The region boasts some of the best trout which are caught in the cold rivers that flow down from the Pyrenees.

In the north of Navarre, which borders the Basque country, the green pastures provide good grazing for the lamb that is very popular here. Las Pocholas serve it as Cordero en Chilindrón, a tasty ragoût of lamb, tomatoes and local white wine. The northern parts of the Rioja wine-growing area extend into the southern regions of Navarre and produce some of the best wines in Spain. The reds are robust and they go well with the full flavour of the regional cooking.

Pamplona is not very far from the sea and local specialities include dishes such as Ajoarriero con Langosta, a combination of cod and lobster; as in the ragoût of lamb, lots of tomatoes, onions and garlic are used. And here again a Rioja red, rather than a white wine, is the right drink.

Good local food and wines and a friendly service awaits the visitor at Las Pocholas.

Right: Lamb in chilindron sauce (p. 81); and casserole of cod and lobster.

Pato en Salsa de Almendras

Duck in Almond Sauce

Serves 4

90 g (3 oz) lard
1 duck liver or 2 chicken livers, chopped
1 onion, sliced
2 cloves garlic, crushed
1.5 kg (3 lb) duck, cut into 8 pieces
¼ cup (1 oz) flour

salt
freshly ground black pepper
4 tomatoes, peeled and chopped
20 blanched almonds, grilled
½ cup (4 fl oz) dry sherry
2 sprigs parsley, finely chopped

1. Heat the lard in a large frying pan and lightly fry the liver. Remove and set aside.
2. Sauté the onion and garlic. Remove and set aside with the liver.
3. Remove most of the fat from the pan, sprinkle the duck pieces with flour, salt and pepper, and fry them in the remaining fat until brown.
4. Add tomatoes, cover the pan and simmer over low heat.
5. In a mortar or food processor, grind the liver, onion and garlic with the almonds into a smooth paste. Mix in the sherry.
6. Add the mixture to the duck, add the parsley and adjust seasoning.
7. Cover and simmer over low heat for 1 to 1¼ hours until duck is tender. To serve arrange the duck pieces on a platter and strain the sauce over.

Conejo de Bosque con Salsa Romera

Rabbit with Romera Sauce

*From **Forn del Nastasi**, Lérida, Catalonia*

Serves 4

¾ cup (6 fl oz) olive oil
1-2 rabbits (depending on size), cut into pieces
salt
freshly ground black pepper
1 onion, finely chopped
2 cloves garlic, crushed
400 g potatoes (14 oz), peeled and diced
½ cup (4 fl oz) brandy

Picada:
½ tablespoon olive oil
2 rabbit livers or chicken livers, chopped
1 clove garlic, crushed
½ cup (2 oz) ground almonds
2 sprigs parsley, chopped
2-3 cups (16-24 fl oz) water

1. In a casserole, heat the oil and fry the rabbit pieces until brown. Season with salt and pepper.
2. Add onion, garlic and potatoes, and fry until onion is soft and transparent. Then add brandy.
3. To make the Picada, heat oil and sauté the rabbit or chicken livers. Chop them and put them in a mortar together with the garlic, almonds and parsley. Pound them thoroughly. This may be done in a food processor.
4. Add the Picada to the casserole. Cook lightly for a few minutes, add water, cover the casserole and simmer over low heat for 1 hour or until the rabbit is tender.

Conejo con Alcachofas

Rabbit with Artichokes

From **Forn del Nastasi**, *Lérida, Catalonia*

Serves 4

¾ cup (6 fl oz) olive oil
1 rabbit, cut into pieces
1 onion, chopped
3 cloves garlic, crushed
2 sprigs parsley
1.5 kg (3 lb) artichokes
juice 1 lemon
3 tablespoons flour
Picada (piquant paste):
¼ teaspoon saffron
1 clove garlic crushed

¼ teaspoon salt
30 g (1 oz) pine nuts, ground
30 g (1 oz) blanched almonds, ground
½ teaspoon cinnamon
1 sprig parsley, chopped
¼-½ cup (2-4 fl oz) dry sherry

1 cup (8 fl oz) dry red wine
½ cup (4 fl oz) stock or water
salt
freshly ground black pepper

1. Heat ½ cup (4 fl oz) of the oil in a casserole and sauté the rabbit pieces, onion, garlic and parsley until they brown lightly.
2. Trim the artichokes, remove tough outside leaves and choke, rub cut surfaces with lemon juice, sprinkle the artichokes with flour and fry them in remaining ¼ cup of oil for a few minutes.
3. Add them to the casserole.
4. To make the Picada, pound all the dry ingredients in a mortar, add sherry and make a fine paste.
5. Add the Picada to the casserole, along with the wine and stock or water, season, cover, and simmer over low flame for 1 hour or until the rabbit is tender.

MEATS

Meat stews are among the best-known Spanish meat dishes. This is not surprising. Traditionally Spain has little that can be considered top-quality grazing land. Dry stony pastures, with a sparse cover of grass, breed tasty but tough meat more suitable for stewing. So in most regions of the country one will find great hearty nourishing stews, and none more famous than Cocido Madrileño or Olla Podrida, the 'Rotten Pot' much beloved by Don Quixote.

Lamb and mutton are good and popular, especially the baby lamb of Old Castile simply roasted and known as Lechazo Asado.

The tough countryside of Extremadura is good breeding ground for goats. Caldereta Extremeña, is kid stewed with dry white wine, garlic, livers and red or green peppers (capsicums). While the Extremadura dish is very tasty, there are regional variations in most parts of Spain.

Pigs are raised throughout the land and chorizo and spicy Spanish hams are world famous. Everybody has his favourite pork dish and mine is Cochinillo Asado de Segovia, tiny succulent and aromatic roast suckling pig, the great speciality of Old Castile; cooked in a special baker's-type oven it is one of the country's great dishes.

When in Spain don't look for beef dishes, as it is a country where bulls are raised for fighting and where the cow or ox are beasts of burden. Veal, however, in a sherry sauce as cooked in Andalusia, is well worth trying.

Spaniards are very frugal and every part of the animal is eaten. Don't be put off by dishes in which offal is used; cooks here are masters at bringing out the best flavour in meat.

Mesón de Rastro, Ávila, Old Castile

Ávila presents an imposing and unique sight to anyone approaching the town, for it is encircled by the oldest and best-preserved mediaeval walls and defence towers in Europe. Despite the passing of time, Ávila retains a quaint and romantic character of the past.

Mesón de Rastro is built right against these walls. Its colourful facade faces one of the many little squares that are scattered through the town.

Ávila is popular among tourists, who are attracted by its unique appearance. At the restaurant simple local dishes can be found on the menu: the trout is from the nearby Tormes river; and spicy sausages and tasty pork are house specialities.

Right: *Clockwise from bottom left: shoulder of pork with chorizos; beans, chorizo and pig's trotters (p. 89); trout stuffed with ham and the best-known dish of the region, roasted suckling pig.*

Caldereta Extremeña

Baby Lamb Stew

*From **Parador Nacional 'Via de la Plata'**, Mérida, Extremadura*

Serves 6-8

2 kg (4 lb) baby lamb, cut into pieces
salt
1 tablespoon paprika
3 bay leaves
250 g (8 oz) lamb liver

2 cups (16 fl oz) dry white wine
2 cloves garlic, crushed
3 slices bread fried in oil, cut into pieces

1. In a bowl combine meat, salt, paprika, bay leaves, liver and wine. Refrigerate for 12 hours.
2. Transfer to a casserole, bring to the boil, cover and simmer over low heat for 1½ hours.
3. Take out the liver, cut it into small pieces and put it in a mortar or food processor, add garlic and bread and purée it to a paste.
4. Add the paste to the lamb, season and cook over low heat for 10 minutes. Serve hot.

Ternasco Asado Aragonés

Roast Baron of Lamb

*From **El Cachirulo**, Zaragoza, Aragón*

Serves 4

6 cloves garlic, crushed
salt
30 g (1 oz) lard
1.5 kg (3 lb) baron of baby lamb
1 kg (2 lb) potatoes, peeled and sliced

1 cup (8 fl oz) boiling water
4 tablespoons olive oil
2 sprigs rosemary, chopped
2 sprigs parsley, chopped
2 cups (16 fl oz) dry white wine

1. Preheat the oven to 220°C (425°F/Gas 7).
2. Mix half of the garlic with the salt and lard and rub it on the lamb.
3. Put the potatoes in the bottom of a baking dish and place the lamb on top, add the water and bake it in the preheated oven for 20 minutes.
4. In a mortar, crush the remainder of the garlic with the oil, rosemary, parsley and some salt. Add the wine and mix well.
5. Pour this mixture over the lamb and potatoes and continue baking for a further 30 to 40 minutes until the lamb is golden brown and the potatoes are cooked. To serve, arrange the potatoes on a platter and place the lamb on top. Spoon the cooking juices over the dish.

Caldereta de Cordero

Lamb Casserole

From **Casa Duque**, *Segovia, Old Castle*

Serves 6

½ cup (4 fl oz) olive oil
1 onion, finely chopped
4 cloves garlic, crushed (use according
   to taste)
2 kg (4 lb) meat from a shoulder of
   lamb cut into 5 cm (2 in) cubes
salt
½ hot pepper, chopped

4 red or green peppers (capsicums),
   seeded and chopped
4 cloves
1 tablespoon paprika
2 cups (16 fl oz) dry white wine
2 sprigs fresh herbs, chopped
4 cups (1 litre) water or stock

1. In a casserole, heat the oil and sauté the onion and garlic.
2. Add meat, salt, hot pepper, red or green peppers (capsicums), cloves, paprika, wine, herbs and water.
3. Simmer for 1 hour or until lamb is tender. Adjust seasoning and serve in individual ceramic bowls called casuela de barro.

Cordero en Chilindron

Lamb in Chilindron Sauce

From **'Las Pocholas', Hostal del Rey Noble**, *Pamplona, Navarre*

Serves 6

1 cup (8 fl oz) olive oil
4 onions, finely chopped
1 clove garlic, crushed
1 kg (2 lb) tomatoes, peeled and
   chopped
1.5 kg (3 lb) lamb from the
   forequarter, cut into pieces

3 red or green peppers (capsicums),
   seeded and chopped
2 cups (16 fl oz) dry white wine
salt
freshly ground black pepper

1. Heat half of the oil in a casserole and sauté 2 of the onions and the garlic until onions are soft and transparent.
2. Add the tomatoes and simmer over low heat for 20 minutes. Cool.
3. Rub through a sieve, set aside.
4. In the casserole, heat the remaining oil and sauté the remaining onions.
5. Add the meat and chopped peppers, and fry until meat starts to brown.
6. Add wine, the tomato-onion-garlic sauce and seasoning. Cover and simmer over low heat for 1 hour.

Cordero Lechal Asado

Roast Suckling Lamb

*From **Casa Duque**, Segovia, Old Castile*

Serves 6

½ side of baby lamb, cut into
   6 portions
salt
freshly ground black pepper
1½ cups (12 fl oz) water

1½ cups (12 fl oz) dry white wine
2 cloves garlic, crushed
2 sprigs thyme, chopped

1. Preheat the oven to 200°C (400°F/Gas 6).
2. Place the lamb pieces in a baking dish, sprinkle with salt and pepper, and add the water.
3. Bake in the preheated oven for 30 minutes.
4. Add wine, garlic and thyme, turn the meat, and return to oven for 45 minutes. Baste occasionally.
5. Serve hot with cooking liquid, and with fried potatoes and lettuce salad.

Casa Duque, Segovia, Old Castile

Segovia is a very hospitable town and boasts many good restaurants. Traditional dishes are the Cochinillo Asado de Segovia, roast suckling pig, and the roast suckling lamb which are particularly well prepared. In general the food is Castilian.

At the Casa Duque I have eaten some of the best food that I found during my journey through Spain. The Duque family has run the restaurant since 1895, and the son of the present owner is a fourth-generation innkeeper – quite a family tradition. Casa Duque serves many of the local specialities.

The Sopa Castellana is a hearty combination of ham, chorizo, (the spicy sausage) and eggs, a meal in itself. Most of the other dishes on the menu are very filling – I guess a characteristic of Castilian cooking. A walk through the town is one way of settling such rich food.

Segovia is among the most attractive Spanish towns. Situated at the confluence of two rivers, it rises high above its immediate surroundings. Its history spans two thousand years. The Roman aqueduct is well preserved and even today still performs its original function. Ancient churches, the houses of noble families and narrow winding streets contribute to the romantic feeling of the town.

Some 3 kilometres along the road past the aqueduct, and overlooking the town from its elevated position, the modern Parador Nacional is one of the most comfortable and impressive hotels I have ever visited.

Right: The host of Casa Duque proudly displays some of the traditional local dishes. Clockwise from bottom left: trout with ham (p. 60); lamb casserole (p. 81); beans, chorizo and pig's trotters, and Castillian soup (p. 21).

Cordero a la Pastoril

Boiled Lamb Shepherd's Style

*From **Restaurant Sevilla**, Granada, Andalusia*

Serves 4

1 kg (2 lb) boned leg of lamb, cut into pieces
¼ cup (2 fl oz) olive oil
⅓ cup (2½ fl oz) vinegar
2 cloves garlic, crushed

1 teaspoon dried oregano
1 teaspoon paprika
pinch cayenne pepper
2 cups (16 fl oz) water
salt

1. Sauté the meat in the oil until brown all round.
2. Combine the meat and the remaining ingredients in a casserole, and simmer over low heat for 1½ hours.

Judiones de la Granja Duque

Broad Beans and Meat Stew

*From **Casa Duque**, Segovia, Old Castile*

Serves 8

8 cups (2 litres) water
750 g (1½ lb) broad beans, soaked overnight
4 pig's trotters
2 chorizo (spicy pork sausage)
2 blood pudding sausages
100 g (3½ oz) bacon, roughly chopped
1 onion, cut into quarters
1 clove garlic
2 bay leaves
salt

Sofrito:
½ cup (4 fl oz) olive oil
2 onions, finely chopped
2 cloves garlic, crushed
3 tomatoes, peeled and chopped
1 tablespoon paprika

1. In a casserole combine all ingredients except those for the Sofrito. Cover, bring to the boil, then simmer over very low heat for 2 hours.
2. To make the Sofrito, heat the oil in a frying pan, add the onions and garlic, cover and sauté over low heat for 15 minutes, stirring occasionally.
3. Add tomatoes and paprika and sauté for a further 10 minutes.
4. Add the Sofrito to the casserole and continue simmering for 1 further hour.
5. Serve from the casserole with the meat arranged on top.

84

Lacón con Grelos

Pickled Shoulder of Pork with Cabbage

From **Anexo Vilas**, *Santiago de Compostela, Galicia*

Delicatessen shops sell cooked pickled shoulder or loin of pickled pork which may be used in this dish.

Serves 8

1.5 kg (3 lb) boneless shoulder or loin
  of pickled pork
8 whole large potatoes, peeled
½ cabbage, roughly chopped (the
  original recipe called for kale)

4 small chorizo (spicy pork sausage)
freshly ground black pepper
2-3 cups (16-24 fl oz) water

1. Place the meat in a large saucepan, cover with water, bring to the boil and simmer over low heat for 2 hours. This should remove excessive salt.
2. Discard the water. Add potatoes, cabbage, chorizo, pepper and fresh water. Cover and simmer over low heat for 1 hour.
3. To serve, cut the meat into slices and arrange them with the cabbage, chorizo and potatoes in the casserole.

Jarrete Guisado

Veal Knuckle Stew

From **Anexo Vilas**, *Santiago de Compostela, Galicia*

Serves 4

2 veal knuckles, cut into 5 cm (2 in)
  pieces
1 cup (8 fl oz) dry white wine
3 cloves garlic, crushed (or less, to
  taste)
salt

freshly ground black pepper
½ cup (4 fl oz) olive oil
8-12 small, whole onions, peeled
8-12 small, whole new potatoes,
  peeled

1. Marinate the meat overnight in a mixture of wine, garlic, salt and pepper.
2. Wipe the meat dry, set the marinade aside. Heat the oil in a casserole, add the meat and brown it on all sides. Add the onions and continue cooking until onions are soft and transparent.
3. Preheat the oven to 180°C (350°F /Gas 4).
4. Add the marinade, cover, and simmer for 45 minutes.
5. Add the potatoes, cover, and cook in preheated oven for a further 45 minutes. Serve hot straight out of the casserole.

Olla Barreixada

Chicken Casserole with Meatballs

*From **Forn del Nastasi**, Lérida, Catalonia*

Serves 4-6

¾ cup (6 fl oz) water
250 g (8 oz) chicken meat
1 lamb shank
250 g (8 oz) dried beans, soaked
  overnight
1 ham bone
1 pig's trotter
1 veal knuckle
¼ cabbage, shredded
250 g (8 oz) potatoes, peeled and
  diced
100 g (3½ oz) black pudding sausage

Pelota (meatballs):
200 g (6½ oz) minced lamb and pork
2 slices soaked bread, squeezed dry
2 sprigs parsley, finely chopped
1 clove garlic, crushed
1 egg, lightly beaten
salt
freshly ground black pepper
100 g (3½ oz) egg noodles
60 g (2 oz) rice
¼ teaspoon saffron

1. Put the water in the casserole, add chicken, lamb, beans and the bones. Cook for 1 hour.
2. Add cabbage, potatoes and black pudding and cook for 30 minutes.
3. In the meantime, make the Pelota (meatballs). In a bowl, combine minced meat, bread, parsley, garlic, egg, salt and pepper. Mix well and form the mixture into 4 cm (1½ in) balls.
4. To the casserole, add the Pelota, noodles, rice and saffron and simmer over low heat for 20 to 30 minutes until rice is cooked. If necessary, add more water.
5. Season to taste, let it stand for 10 minutes and serve from the casserole.

Hostería Nacional 'Del Comendador', Cáceres, Extremadura
Extremadura and in particular the Cáceres district are closely connected with the Spanish conquest of the Americas. In the nearby town of Guadalupe the first Indians brought back from the New World were baptised.

It was the wealth that flowed across the Atlantic that built the many fine churches, proud mansions and palaces of Cáceres.

It is an attractive, romantic town and a stroll through the narrow winding streets is very rewarding. The old quarter of the town is surrounded by walls and fortified towers; and it is not difficult to imagine the busy life of people who prospered here five or six hundred years ago.

The Hostería Nacional is situated in one of the houses of the nobility. Local food and wines are offered in pleasant tranquil surroundings. The countryside around Cáceres produces good lamb and pigs, and the hams and sausages enjoy a well-deserved reputation for quality and strong flavour. The region is good hunting country and many of the local dishes include pheasant and partridge.

***Right:** Clockwise from bottom left: Rich fruit cake of Guadalupe; Sweetmeats made from syrup and eggs (p. 93); pickled trout (p. 61) and skewered pork.*

Olla Podrida Catalana

Catalan Stew

Serves 8

100 g (3½ oz) lard
1.5 kg (3 lb) chicken, cut in pieces
250 g (8 oz) shoulder meat of lamb, cut into pieces
125 g (4 oz) pickled pork, cut in pieces
125 g (4 oz) black pudding sausage, sliced
125 g (4 oz) chorizo (spicy pork sausage), sliced
16 cups (4 litres) water
1 cup (6 oz) chickpeas, soaked overnight

250 g (8 oz) minced beef
salt
freshly ground black pepper
¼ teaspoon saffron
3 sprigs parsley, chopped
1 egg, lightly beaten
2 onions, chopped
4 potatoes, sliced
¼ cabbage, shredded
250 g (8 oz) egg noodles

1. Heat the lard in a large saucepan and brown the chicken, lamb and pork.
2. Add the black pudding, chorizo and water, bring to the boil and simmer over low heat for 2 hours.
3. Add chickpeas and simmer for another hour.
4. Mix minced beef, salt, pepper, saffron, parsley and egg. Make into small meatballs.
5. Add meatballs, onions, potatoes and cabbage to the pot and cook for a further hour.
6. Drain off the liquid into another saucepan and cook the noodles in it, season and serve it as a soup. Serve the drained meat and vegetables as the main course.

Callos a la Gallega

Tripe and Chickpeas

From Anexo Vilas, Santiago de Compostela, Galicia

Serves 6

30 g (1 oz) lard
2 onions, chopped
1-2 cloves garlic, crushed
1 tablespoon flour
1 tablespoon paprika
½ teaspoon cumin
salt

8 cups (2 litres) water
1 kg (2 lb) tripe, cut into pieces
1 boned shoulder of lamb, cut into pieces
2 chorizo (spicy pork sausage), sliced
500 g (1 lb) chickpeas, soaked overnight

1. In a casserole, heat the lard and sauté the onions and garlic until onions are soft and transparent.
2. Add flour, paprika, cumin, salt and water, stir well, and cook for 5 minutes.
3. Add the tripe, cover and cook for 1½ hours.
4. Add the lamb and chorizo slices and cook for 30 minutes.
5. Add chickpeas and cook for a further hour. Season and serve directly from casserole.

Judías del Barco de Ávila

Beans, Chorizo and Pig's Trotters

*From **Mesón del Rastro**, Ávila, Old Castile*

Serves 4

¼ cup (2 fl oz) olive oil
2 onions, chopped
1 clove garlic, crushed
2 red or green peppers (capsicums),
    seeded and roughly chopped
2 chorizo (spicy pork sausage), sliced

4 pig's trotters
salt
freshly ground black pepper
4 cups (1 litre) water
375 g (12 oz) dried beans, soaked
    overnight

1. Heat the oil in a casserole or saucepan and sauté the onion and garlic until onions are soft and transparent.
2. Add chopped peppers, chorizo slices, pig's trotters, seasoning and cook for 10 minutes, stirring occasionally.
3. Add water and beans, cover, and simmer over low heat for 1½ to 2 hours until the trotters are cooked.
4. Serve out of the casserole with some of the chorizo slices and the trotters arranged on top.

Mollejas de Ternera

Sweetbreads in Sauce

*From **Casa Duque**, Segovia, Old Castile*

Serves 6

½ cup (4 fl oz) olive oil
2-3 cloves garlic, crushed
800 g (26 oz) sweetbreads, blanched,
    cleaned and cut into pieces
1 tablespoon flour
2 tomatoes, peeled and chopped
1 tablespoon tomato paste

¼ cup chopped hot pepper
3 sprigs parsley, chopped
2 bay leaves
½ cup (4 fl oz) dry sherry
1 cup (8 fl oz) water
salt

1. Preheat the oven to 200°C (400°F/Gas 6).
2. In a frying pan, heat the oil and lightly fry the garlic, add sweetbreads, sprinkle with flour, and sauté until lightly brown. Add tomatoes, tomato paste, hot pepper, parsley, bay leaves, sherry, water and salt to taste.
3. Transfer to a casserole and cook in the preheated oven for 10 minutes. Serve directly from the dish.

DESSERTS AND CAKES

The Spanish people have a reputation of possessing a very sweet tooth, yet they are not great dessert eaters and usually prefer fresh fruit in season or cheese to finish off a meal. It is therefore not surprising to find that the sweets repertoire is limited.

However, on festive days (mostly devoted to a local patron saint) the occasional dessert appears on the table. Frequently it is a cake which doubles as a dessert to finish off the meal. Among the most famous of that type is the almond pastry cake *cum* dessert in honour of St James, the Tarta de Santiago, a speciality of Galicia.

Spain shares with Portugal a predilection for custards. The flan or caramel custard is a favourite throughout the land. In Catalonia it is the Crema Catalana, made with egg yolks, milk and covered with burnt sugar. Needless to say, the speciality of Valencia includes the flavour of the famous Valencia orange.

The Moors introduced almonds and various sweets made with these nuts. Almond tarts (Bartolillos) and marzipan are a legacy from those far-distant days. In a country where rice is a staple, rich rice puddings are popular. The one I tasted in Segovia had a delicate scent of lemon and orange peel which was pleasant in contrast to the heady aroma of cinnamon with which it was sprinkled.

Fruit, in addition to being eaten fresh, is also popular when in its dried form. Dried figs and rice (Higos y Arroz) with melted chocolate and whipped cream is a lush delicious dessert.

After using the egg yolks in custards, there is a lot of egg white left. One of the many ways of using up the egg whites is in Manzanas Asadas, Asturian baked apples, which are cored, filled with apricot jam covered with meringue and baked.

As with most Spanish food, regional differences are reflected in a large variety of pastries, cakes and biscuits.

Right: In the former chapel of the converted convent, laid out on the long refrectory table is a house speciality of the Parador Nacional Via de la Plata, the Convent Tart.

Arroz con Leche Caldoso

Rice Pudding

From **Casa Duque**, *Segovia, Old Castile*

Serves 6

4 cups (1 litre) milk
1 teaspoon grated lemon peel
1 teaspoon grated orange peel

100 g (3⅓ oz) rice
150 g (5 oz) sugar
½ teaspoon cinnamon

1. In a saucepan, heat the milk, lemon peel and orange peel. When it boils, add rice and, stirring occasionally, cook over low heat for 25 minutes.
2. Add the sugar and simmer for 10 minutes.
3. Cool, and serve cold sprinkled with cinnamon.

Tarta de Santiago

Tart of St James

From **Anexo Vilas**, *Santiago de Compostela, Galicia*

Serves 6-8

8 eggs
2 cups (1 lb) sugar
2⅓ cups (9½ oz) flour
250 g (8 oz) butter, softened

1 cup (8 fl oz) water
4½ cups (1 lb) ground almonds
1 teaspoon grated lemon peel
icing (confectioners') sugar

1. Preheat the oven to 180°C (350°F/Gas 4).
2. Cream the eggs with the sugar until pale yellow, light and fluffy.
3. Add flour, butter and water. Beat in an electric beater for 15 minutes.
4. Add almonds and lemon peel.
5. Pour the mixture into a round, greased baking tin and bake in the preheated oven for 30 to 40 minutes until done.
6. Serve sprinkled with icing sugar and cut into wedges.

Melocotón con Vino

Peaches in Wine

From **El Cachirulo**, *Zaragoza, Aragón*

Serves 4

4-8 slipstone/freestone peaches, peeled and halved
2 cups (16 fl oz) dry red wine

¼ cup (2 oz) sugar
1 stick cinnamon, 5 cm (2 in) long
½ cup (4 fl oz) brandy

1. Mix wine, sugar, cinnamon and brandy until sugar is dissolved.
2. Place peaches in a bowl, pour the mixture over the peaches, cover the bowl with plastic film, and refrigerate for 4 days.
3. Serve cold in individual dessert bowls.

Tocinillo de Cielo

Sweetmeats made from Syrup and Eggs

From **Hosteria Nacional 'Del Comendador'**, *Cáceres, Extremadura*

Serves 6

1½ cups (12 oz) sugar
½ cup (4 fl oz) water

11 egg yolks
1 whole egg

1. Preheat the oven to 160°C (325°F/Gas 3).
2. Dissolve all but 3 tablespoons of sugar in the water.
3. Bring the dissolved sugar to the boil and cook until the syrup forms a thread. Cool slightly.
4. Sprinkle the remaining 3 tablespoons of sugar on the bottom of a large rectangular baking tin at least 3 cm (1¼ in) deep, place over heat until the sugar caramelises. Set aside.
5. Place the yolks and egg in a bowl and, either by hand or with a mixer, whip until the eggs start to cream, keep beating and slowly incorporate the warm syrup until the mixture is thick.
6. Carefully pour the mixture into the baking dish. Cover the dish with foil, place it into another dish which is slightly larger and is filled with boiling water. Place in the preheated oven and cook until the mixture sets.
7. Cool, and refrigerate. To serve, cut into slices about 10 x 10 cm (4 x 4 in), and serve on individual plates.

Higos y Arroz

Figs and Rice

Serves 6

½ cup (3 oz) rice
4 cups (1 litre) milk
½ cup (4 oz) sugar
2 eggs, beaten
12 dried figs, chopped

grated rind of 1 lemon
juice of 1 lemon
½ cup (4 fl oz) melted chocolate
½ cup (4 fl oz) cream, whipped

1. In a double boiler, cook the rice, milk and sugar until the rice is soft.
2. Add eggs and chopped figs. Continue cooking and stirring until the mixture thickens, add lemon rind and juice.
3. Butter and sprinkle with sugar 6 individual small moulds or soufflé dishes. Spoon the mixture into the dishes. Cool, and refrigerate.
4. Unmould, and serve with melted chocolate and whipped cream.

Faramayas

Deep Fried Biscuits

*From **Anexo Vilas**, Santiago de Compostela, Galicia*

Serves 6-8

2 cups (8 oz) flour
¼ cup (2 oz) caster (powdered) sugar
grated rind of 1 lemon
50 g (1½ oz) butter

3 tablespoons brandy
1 tablespoon water
oil
icing (confectioners') sugar

1. In a bowl, mix flour, caster sugar and lemon rind.
2. Gently rub in the butter, add brandy and water, mix in with minimum of kneading. Wrap up in foil and refrigerate for 1½ hours.
3. Roll out thinly, cut into 5 cm (2 in) squares, place on a floured tray, cover and refrigerate.
4. Deep fry in hot oil. Drain, dust with icing sugar, and serve either hot or cold.

Right: The Cathedral, Seville.

Manzanas Asadas

Asturian Baked Apples

Serves 4

4 large cooking apples, cored
½ cup (4 fl oz) sweet dessert sherry
⅓ cup (3 oz) sugar
¼ teaspoon vanilla essence

2 egg whites
5 teaspoons apricot jam or apricot jelly

1. Preheat the oven to 180°C (350°F /Gas 4).
2. Place the apples in a buttered baking dish, sprinkle them with the sherry and some of the sugar. Bake in the preheated oven for 10 minutes.
3. In a bowl, add the vanilla to the egg whites and add all but a tablespoon of sugar. Whip until stiff.
4. Place a spoonful of apricot jam in the core hole of the apple and spread some on the surface of each.
5. Place an equal amount of the whipped egg white on each apple, sprinkle with the remaining tablespoon of sugar. Bake them in the oven for a further 10 to 15 minutes until apples are tender and the meringue is brown.

Flan de Naranja

Orange Custard

*From **Restaurant Viveros**, Valencia*

Serves 4

¾ cup (6 fl oz) freshly squeezed orange juice, strained
¾ cup (6½ oz) sugar

⅓ cup (2½ fl oz) water
8 egg yolks
1 whole egg

1. Preheat the oven to 180°C (350°F /Gas 4).
2. Stir the juice, sugar and water until the sugar dissolves.
3. Bring it to the boil and simmer for 10 minutes. Cool.
4. Lightly beat the egg yolks and egg together.
5. Mix syrup and eggs, and pour it into a mould.
6. Place the mould in a dish filled with hot water, cover with foil and cook in the preheated oven for 30 minutes until custard sets.
7. Cool, and if desired refrigerate, and serve turned out on to a platter.

Pastel a la Gallega

Galician Cake

*From **Anexo Vilas**, Santiago de Compostela, Galicia*

Makes a 21 x 11 x 6 cm (8½ x 4½ x 2½ in) tin loaf

¾ cup (3 oz) flour
1 tablespoon baking powder (or use
   100 g (3½ oz) self-raising flour
   instead of the plain flour and baking
   powder)
⅓ cup (3 oz) sugar
5 tablespoons oil

1 tablespoon milk
2 egg yolks
grated rind of 1 lemon
juice of 1 lemon
2 egg whites, stiffly whipped

1. Preheat the oven to 180°C (350°F/Gas 4).
2. In a bowl, sieve the flour and the baking powder (or the self-raising flour), add sugar, oil, milk, egg yolks, rind and lemon juice. Mix well together.
3. Fold in the egg whites.
4. Butter the tin and pour in the mixture.
5. Bake for 30 minutes in the preheated oven.
6. Place cake on cake grid, and allow it to cool. Serve sliced.

Torrijas

French Toast

*From **El Cachirulo**, Zaragoza, Aragón*

Serves 4

8 slices white bread
1 cup (8 fl oz) milk
½ teaspoon cinnamon
2 eggs, lightly beaten

oil, for frying
3 tablespoons sugar mixed with
   ½ teaspoon cinnamon

1. Briefly soak each bread slice in milk mixed with cinnamon, then dip the slice in the beaten egg.
2. Fry in hot oil until brown.
3. Serve hot, sprinkled with cinnamon sugar.

Buñuelos de Plátano

Banana Fritters

Serves 4

1 cup (4 oz) flour
1 egg, lightly beaten
15 g (½ oz) melted butter
½ cup (4 fl oz) milk
1 egg white, beaten stiff

6 teaspoons (1 oz) sugar
3 tablespoons brandy
6 bananas, thickly sliced
oil, for frying
icing (confectioners') sugar

1. Using half of the flour, mix it with the egg, butter and milk to make a smooth batter. Refrigerate for 1 hour.
2. In the meantime, mix the sugar and brandy until sugar dissolves. Pour it over the bananas in a bowl, set aside for 30 minutes, turn to make sure that all slices are well marinated.
3. Remove the bananas from the marinade, drain them, dust them in flour, dip them in the batter and fry them in 8-10 cm (3-4 in) of hot oil until golden brown on both sides.
4. Let the oil drain off, and serve them warm, sprinkled with icing sugar.

Bartolillos

Almond Tarts

250 g (8 oz) deep-frozen puff pastry, defrosted
¼ cup (1 oz) blanched almonds, toasted and crushed
⅔ cup (5 oz) caster (powdered) sugar

⅔ cup (5 fl oz) water
2 egg yolks, lightly beaten
1 egg, lightly beaten for glazing

1. Preheat the oven to 200°C (400°F/Gas 6).
2. Roll out the pastry as thin as possible, cut it into circles to fit a tartlet tray. Reserve a thin strip of pastry for decoration.
3. Grease the tray and line the moulds with the pastry circles.
4. Mix the almonds, sugar, water and yolks.
5. Fill the tartlets with this mixture.
6. Cut a thin strip of pastry and make a cross over each tartlet.
7. With a pastry brush, glaze the pastry with the beaten egg.
8. Bake in the preheated oven for 15 to 20 minutes until pastry is golden brown.

Right: Some of the best food in Spain comes from Andalusia. Restaurante Sevilla in Granada specialises in dishes of that province. Clockwise from bottom left: Omelette with lamb's brains (p. 41); Mixed salad Sevilla (p. 44); Boiled lamb shepherd's style (p. 84) and ham with beans.

Restaurante Sevilla, Granada, Andalusia

The name Granada evokes romantic images. The Moorish castles, the palace of the Alhambra with its beautiful court-yards, the breathtaking delicacy of the Generalife gardens, all combine into dreamlike experience.

The Alhambra looks down on the town; and both are a magnificent sight when viewed against the snowcapped mountains of the Sierra Nevada. In the narrow winding streets of this historic town one can find many bars and tavernas which serve Andalusian food. The food in general is light and several local dishes reveal their Arab origin.

One of these tavernas is the Restaurante Sevilla. Here, at the bar, tapas of local olives and the famous Jamón Serrano de Granada, tasty ham cured in the crisp air of the Sierra, are served.

Sevillana salad, a mixture of red peppers, onion rings, tomatoes, olives, garlic and cooked rice, is eaten at the Sevilla with a dish such as the Tortilla al Sacromonte, an omelette with lambs' brains, peas and ham – almost a meal in itself. In another of the restaurant's specialities, Cordero a la Pastoril, the fragrance of oregano and sweet peppers combine to give the lamb a delicious flavour.

PORTUGAL
INTRODUCTION

The food of Portugal is the food of farmers and fishermen. Basically simple yet nourishing, it takes advantage of what happens to be locally available.

It follows the seasons, feast days and other important events in local life. No part of the country is far from the sea so fresh seafood is available in all but the most remote and inaccessible mountain regions.

Life in Portugal is closely linked with the sea and it is therefore not surprising that the fishermen enjoy the reputation of being masters of their trade. Since time immemorial, Portuguese fishermen have sailed the stormy Atlantic to the Grand Banks off Newfoundland to bring back a rich catch of cod. In its salt-dried form of bacalhau, it is prepared in countless ways throughout the country. Originally it was the food of the poor; now it is universal and very popular, and it is indeed the national dish of Portugal.

Internationally, port wine is without doubt, the most famous product of the country, followed by another wine, the lush and rich-tasting Madeira. It is interesting to note that neither wine plays a part in the indigenous regional cooking. The sophistication of cooking with such luxurious wines has no place in the kitchen of the men of the land and sea.

Many aspects have influenced Portuguese cooking. Portuguese explorers in the East Indies, the Far East and in the New World, and their discoveries of new types of food, have left their mark. In the south of the country and on the island of Madeira, Moorish and African influence can be detected, while Spanish cooking has also had its influence, especially in the north, where dishes similar to those in Galicia across the border can be found.

In general, herbs and spices, even curry, are widely used. Salt-dried cod is one of the staples and it is hard to imagine Portuguese cooking without it. Pork is the most popular meat which, in view of the meagre pastures, is easily understandable. This also explains the Portuguese predilection for veal. Beef and lamb, which requires extensive pastures for long periods of time, are scarce. There are plenty of chickens and they are prepared in many ways.

Eggs are plentiful and are used extensively, especially the egg yolks, which can be found in many delicious sweets and desserts – such as the rich yellow custard called Pudim.

Fresh and dried figs, nuts and chestnuts as well as rice are part of popular cooking. Olive oil rather than animal fats is used. Lemon juice is frequently sprinkled on meat.

Bread plays an important part, especially in the Açordas, the bread soups which are typically Portuguese. These are made with softened bread, oil, crushed garlic, vegetables and chicken or pork. Along the coastline you can find fish or shellfish Açorda.

Portugal's cuisine can be divided into seafood and mountain cooking. Along the coast, seafood dishes predominate. In many of these the fishermen's wives use up the small fish caught in the nets, while the larger fish are sold.

In the mountainous inland areas, in addition to the Açordas, other thick soups, stews and heavy dishes are generally prepared. The three northern provinces of Minho, Trás-os-Montes e Alto Douro and Douro Litoral are mostly rugged and poor, but the cooking is good and in many respects similar to the cooking of Galicia to the north. One of the best-known Portuguese soups, now eaten throughout the country, comes from this region; it is the Caldo Verde, a tasty green broth made from kale and potatoes. By coincidence also, vinho verde, the popular green wine, is produced here. Green does not refer to its colour but to the fact that the grapes are pressed before they are fully ripe; the wine, white or red, has a tart, light and refreshing flavour, is low in alcohol and is slightly effervescent.

It is also in this part of the country where the grapes are cultivated to produce Portugal's most famous wine, the port of Oporto. Portugal's second largest city, Oporto is a prosperous seaport and wine merchants' town; it is also known for a high standard of cooking.

Most representative of coastal cooking is the province of Beira Litoral. North of the city of Aveiro and stretching to Ovar is a large lagoon, rich in fish. Its peaceful and picturesque painted fishing boats bring home a rich catch.

The Caldeirada, a fish and shellfish stew, is prepared all along the Portuguese coast; that of Aveiro combines salt-water and freshwater fish. It includes mullet, freshwater eel, red snapper, sole, octopus, crabs, prawns, sometimes squid, clams and mussels, all cooked in a thick sauce with cumin, parsley, coriander, sliced carrots and onions. After such a rich-sounding combination, Ovos Moles or 'soft eggs', also a speciality of Aveiro, may be the right dish to finish off the meal.

Lisbon is to the south and like most capital cities it offers food from all over the country. However, it also has specialities it calls its own. Being a fishing port, you will find a large number of fish specialities, in particular fish soups, such as Lisbon's own version of the Caldeirada.

Today there is no suggestion that Algarve, the southern coastal region of Portugal, is 'the land beyond'. One of Europe's popular summer holiday resorts, its mild climate, natural beauty, the picturesque coastline, its romantic past, and (last but not least) its delicious food, attracts visitors from all corners of the world.

The regional food here is produced from many elements. The waters of the Atlantic yield a rich harvest of fish and other seafood. Sardinhas Assadas, fresh sardines, are grilled on open charcoal fires, eaten with salad and washed down with local wines.

Some of the best fruit and vegetables come from this region. It is also well known for its sweets and cakes, many of them of Arab origin, combining almonds, sugar and eggs.

To the north of Algarve is the region of Alentejo, the largest province but not as well known as its southern neighbour. Here the climate is severe – hot in summer and cold in winter – with plain landscapes which hold few attractions for the traveller. It is wheat-growing country and the local bread is very tasty; the famous bread soups of Portugal, the Açordas, started in this area. In addition to wheat fields, there is a lot of grazing country producing very good lamb and, from the milk, a number of fine cheeses. In summer a local version of the Gazpacho gives welcome refreshment from the summer heat. Olives and almond trees dot the landscape, while orchards, especially plum trees, produce full-flavoured fruit, most of which is used in high-quality preserves.

A look at Portuguese food would be incomplete without a glimpse across the water to the sunny island of Madeira. Its famous rich wine, so highly regarded by connoisseurs, is not used in local cooking; the few dishes that do include Madeira are mostly of French origin.

On the island the mild climate all year round favours fruit, flowers and vegetables. In addition to the grapes that produce the Madeira wine, there are bananas, avocados, chestnuts, custard apples, passionfruit and many others grown in this tiny paradise. Needless to say there is a great deal of fish and first-class seafood. Indeed, as on mainland Portugal, the best dishes of Madeira are those using ingredients from the sea.

SOUPS

The best known of Portuguese soups and one that is eaten throughout the country is the Caldo Verde. Made from finely shredded kale or cabbage, it is representative of local soups which are of peasant origin.

The Açorda of Alentejo is another typical example, in which in a simple way the flavouring of garlic, oil and herbs is combined with boiling water and bread.

Portugal has its own version of Gazpacho which is very tasty and refreshing during summer and is vaguely related to the Spanish dish.

I still think that Portuguese fish soups are the best, and a good fisherman's stew is always welcome.

Gazpacho à Portuguêsa

Portuguese Gazpacho

Serves 4

1 red or green pepper (capsicum), seeded and finely chopped

6 tomatoes, peeled, seeded and finely chopped

1 clove garlic, crushed

¼ cup (2 fl oz) vinegar

¼ cup (2 fl oz) olive oil

salt

1¼ cups (10 fl oz) iced water or iced tomato juice

125 g (4 oz) paprika sausage, finely chopped

1 cucumber, peeled, seeded and diced

fried sippets made from 4 slices of bread

1. Combine chopped pepper, tomatoes, garlic, vinegar, oil, salt and water (or tomato juice), and refrigerate for 2 to 3 hours.
2. Serve chilled in individual soup bowls, sprinkled with sausage, cucumber and sippets.

Pousada da Ria, Murtosa

The Ria de Aveiro is a peaceful lagoon between Aveiro and Ovar. Richly painted boats with old-fashioned gaff-rigged sails glide unhurried over the calm waters, their cargo a rich catch of fish, a load of salt or green algae. The salt is used in preserving cod that is brought back from distant Newfoundland. A large portion of the very popular bacalhau is dried in the region. However, fresh fish and shellfish from the lagoon, as well as freshwater fish such as eel, combine in a thick sauce with cumin, parsley, coriander, carrot and onions to make up the local speciality, the Caldeirada.

The Pousada da Ria, a modern well-appointed hotel, overlooks the quiet seascape of the lagoon. Here the vacationer finds not only tranquility but also a rich and varied cuisine which presents fresh seafood from local waters.

Ovos moles, an egg yolk sugar dessert, originates from this area and is a typically Portuguese way to end a meal.

Right: Clockwise from bottom left: Country baked red porgy (p. 120); grilled skewered kidneys; green salad; fried sardines.

Sopa de Tomate à Alentejana

Alentejo Tomato Soup

Serves 6

175 g (5½ oz) lard
175 g (5½ oz) chouriço (spicy pork sausage), sliced
2 onions, sliced
500 g (1 lb) tomatoes, peeled, seeded and chopped
6 cups (1.5 litres) stock or water

2 bay leaves
1 red or green pepper (capsicum), seeded and roughly chopped
salt
6 slices fresh bread

1. Heat the lard in a saucepan and sauté the sausage and onions until onions are golden brown.
2. Add tomatoes and cook for 5 minutes.
3. Add stock or water, bay leaves, chopped pepper, and salt. Cook for 10 minutes. Serve hot in individual soup bowls, poured over slices of bread.

Canja de Galinha

Chicken Soup with Lemon and Mint

Serves 6-8

1.5 kg (3 lb) chicken
200 g (6½ oz) chicken giblets, chopped
6 cups (1.5 litres) water
2 onions, finely chopped
1 stalk celery, finely chopped
1 teaspoon salt

2 bay leaves
⅔ cup (4 oz) rice
juice 1½ lemons
6-10 mint leaves, finely chopped
freshly ground black pepper

1. Place the chicken in a large saucepan, add giblets, water, onions, celery, salt and bay leaves. Cover and simmer over low heat for 2 hours.
2. Remove the chicken and let it cool. Add rice to the broth and simmer for 20 to 30 minutes, until the rice is soft. Stir occasionally.
3. In the meantime, remove the skin from the chicken and take the meat off the bones. Discard bones and skin.
4. Cut the meat into small strips and add it to the broth, add lemon juice, and serve sprinkled with mint.

Caldo Verde

Cabbage and Potato Broth

From **Pousada de S.Lourenço**, *Manteigas, Serra da Estrela*

The most typical of Portugal's soups. It is made with kale or cabbage, shredded as fine as possible.

Serves 4-6

500 g (1 lb) potatoes, peeled and each cut into quarters
4 cups (1 litre) water
salt
4 tablespoons olive oil

1 onion, finely chopped
250 g (8 oz) cabbage leaves, very finely shredded
freshly ground black pepper

1. Boil the potatoes in salted water until they are soft enough for mashing.
2. Remove the potatoes to a bowl and save the water.
3. Mash the potatoes and return them to the saucepan with the water.
4. Add the oil, onion and cabbage and boil for 3 to 4 minutes. Season and serve hot. Slices of chouriço (a Portuguese spicy pork sausage) may also be cooked in the soup.

Sopa à Alentejana

Bread and Garlic Soup

Serves 4

2 cloves garlic
1 teaspoon coarse salt
4 sprigs fresh coriander, chopped
½ cup (4 fl oz) olive oil

2 cups (16 fl oz) boiling water
4 slices bread, fried in lard
4 poached eggs

1. Grind garlic, salt and coriander in a mortar, or process to a paste in a food processor, and gradually beat in the oil.
2. Pour in the water and mix well.
3. Place a slice of bread in the bottom of each soup bowl, pour the soup over it and put a poached egg on top. In the original recipe, the bread is used fresh.

VEGETABLES

In most Portuguese vegetable dishes, a number of ingredients are combined. Beans of all kinds, fresh or dried, are popular. Broad beans with bacon and sausage are a substantial dish and frequently served as a main course.

It is quite common to combine a number of vegetables together; tomatoes, onions and squashes, for example, make up a popular luncheon dish.

Potatoes are simply boiled and alternate with rice as an accompaniment to most meals.

Mixed Vegetables with Tomatoes and Scrambled Eggs

Serves 4

1 tablespoon olive oil
½ onion, finely chopped
½ clove garlic, crushed
3 tomatoes, peeled, seeded and chopped
salt
freshly ground black pepper

1 potato, peeled and diced
1 carrot, scraped and diced
100 g (3½ oz) green beans, cut into 2.5 cm (1 in) pieces
100 g (3½ oz) cauliflower, broken up into small flowerets
scrambled eggs made from 8 eggs

1. Heat oil and sauté onion and garlic for 5 minutes.
2. Add tomatoes, salt and pepper, and simmer for 20 minutes.
3. Add potato and carrot and cook for 5 minutes.
4. Add beans and cauliflower, and cook for a further 10 minutes.
5. If necessary, season to taste. Serve with hot scrambled eggs.

Pousada S. Bartolomeu, Bragança

It's a long and winding road from Oporto to Bragança. The countryside is sparsely cultivated and the name Trás-os-Montes, 'Beyond the Mountains', conjures the right atmosphere of isolation. Yet along the road local people offer some delicious products: tasty cheeses and ripe aromatic strawberries. And there are lots of chestnut trees and the occasional cork tree with its bright brown trunk.

Bragança is dominated by an old castle and its tall mediaeval tower.

On a hillside facing the castle is the Pousada S. Bartolomeu, a comfortable modern hotel and pleasant resting point after a hectic drive through the mountains. As in most pousadas, local dishes are served. Pork and chestnuts and sausages as well as trout from local rivers are among the regional specialities.

Right: In foreground: marinated roast veal (p. 129). Top left: eel fricassée with egg-lemon sauce (p. 121). Top right: orange roll (p. 138).

Favas à Saloia

Broad Beans, Bacon and Sausage

Serves 4

75 g (2½ oz) lard
1 onion, finely sliced
1 clove garlic, crushed
1 sprig coriander or parsley, chopped
2 slices bacon, chopped
250 g (8 oz) chouriço (spicy pork sausage), chopped

1 tablespoon sugar
salt
500 g (1 lb) fresh broad beans
1-2 cups (8-16 fl oz) stock

1. In a casserole, heat the lard and sauté onion and garlic until the onion is soft and transparent.
2. Add coriander or parsley, bacon, chouriço sausage, sugar, salt, beans and enough stock to cover. Cover the casserole and cook for approximately 1 hour or until the beans are cooked.

Favas à Algarvia

Broad Beans with Salami and Ham

Serves 4

1 tablespoon olive oil
1 onion, finely chopped
125 g (4 oz) salami, finely chopped
125 g (4 oz) proscuitto-style ham, sliced
2½ cups (20 fl oz) chicken stock (see p. 140)

500 g (1 lb) fresh broad beans
125 g (4 oz) carrots, sliced
1 tablespoon tomato purée
salt
freshly ground black pepper

1. Heat the oil in a casserole and sauté the onion, salami and ham for 5 minutes.
2. Add stock, beans, carrots, tomato purée and seasoning.
3. Cover and simmer over low heat for 1 hour or until beans and carrots are cooked.

Deep-fried French Beans

Serves 6

500 g (1 lb) French beans
125 g (4 oz) self-raising flour
1 egg
salt

⅔ cup (5½ fl oz) dry white wine
flour
oil for deep frying
freshly ground black pepper

1. String the beans and cook them in boiling salted water until they are almost tender.
2. Make a smooth batter by combining self-raising flour, egg, salt and wine.
3. Dust the beans with flour, dip them in the batter and fry them for 1 to 2 minutes until they are crisp and light brown. Serve immediately, sprinkled with salt and pepper.

FISH

It is natural for a nation of fishermen that the best dishes of Portugal are made with ingredients from the sea.

Today it is difficult to imagine Portuguese cooking without bacalhau, the salt-dried cod. While no place in Portugal is very far from the coast and fresh fish and seafood are available in most parts of the country, bacalhau in many guises is the national dish. For centuries Portuguese fishermen have braved the rough Atlantic Ocean and have sailed thousands of kilometres to the Grand Banks near the Canadian coast of Newfoundland to harvest the rich fishing grounds.

Along the coast of Portugal a traveller will find a great number and variety of seafood dishes. However, there is one that is common to all parts: the Caldeirada, the classic seafood stew. Prepared from fish and shellfish, it is the expression of local culinary imagination. It contains whatever ingredients are locally available and there must be as many versions of that dish as there are fishing villages along the long coastline of Portugal.

At the Pousada da Ria, on the lagoon north of Aveiro, I tasted a local variety which combines fresh and saltwater fish in a rich fish broth.

Some of the best seafood in Portugal is very simply prepared. Fresh sardines grilled over an open fire, eaten with a fresh salad of crisp lettuce and ripe tomatoes, and washed down with a bottle of chilled local white wine, are a great delight.

Pousada de S. Lourenço, Manteigas

After many hairpin bends, the steep road leads to the Pousada de S. Lourenço, 55 km from the old town of Guarda and right in the heart of the Serra da Estrela.

At an altitude of 1280 metres, the cool and fresh climate of the summer attracts many visitors who wish to enjoy the healthy mountain air and tasty specialities of the region. Roast kid is served at the table as Cabrito à Beira and local mountain trout is presented with regional ham. There is a house version of the Caldo Verde and the ever-present bacalhau.

The Pousada has the atmosphere of a ski lodge, which is not surprising as the Serra da Estrela is being developed as a ski resort.

Right: Clockwise from bottom left: trout with ham; Cod S. Laurenço fashion; roasted kid; cabbage and potato broth (p. 105); Portuguese sweet rice (p. 138).

Amêijoas na Cataplana

Clams with Sausage and Ham

A Cataplan is a traditional metal cooking dish with tight-fitting lid. A lidded, heavy casserole may be used.

Serves 4

3 tablespoons oil
4 onions, sliced
1 clove garlic, crushed
1 teaspoon paprika
dash of Tabasco sauce, to taste
freshly ground black pepper
2 tomatoes, peeled, seeded and finely
  chopped

100 g (3½ oz) smoked ham or
  prosciutto, chopped
100 g (3½ oz) chouriço (spicy pork
  sausage), chopped
½ cup (4 fl oz) dry white wine
2 sprigs parsley, finely chopped
36 clams or mussels, washed

1. Heat the oil in a casserole and sauté the onion and garlic until onions are soft and transparent.
2. Add paprika, Tabasco sauce, pepper, tomatoes, ham, chouriço sausage, wine and parsley, and simmer for 10 minutes.
3. Place the clams or mussels on top, cover tightly, and cook over medium heat for 8 to 10 minutes until the shellfish open. Serve immediately.

Bacalhau à Gomes de Sá

Cod with Potatoes, Onions and Black Olives

Serves 6

750 g (1½ lb) dried salt cod
6 potatoes
1¼ cups (10 fl oz) olive oil
4 onions, sliced

1 clove garlic, crushed
24 black olives
6 hard-boiled eggs, cut into quarters
2 sprigs parsley, finely chopped

1. Soak the cod in cold water for 12 hours, changing the water several times.
2. Preheat the oven to 180°C (350°F/Gas 4).
3. Drain the cod and rinse under running water.
4. Put the cod in a saucepan, cover with water and simmer over low heat for 1 hour.
5. Drain, remove skin and bones and, with a fork, flake into pieces. Set aside.
6. Boil the potatoes.
7. Peel and cut the potatoes into slices. Set aside.
8. In a frying pan, heat the oil and sauté the onions and garlic.
9. Grease a casserole and arrange two layers each of potatoes, cod, onions and olives.
10. Bake in the preheated oven for 20 minutes or until brown.
11. Serve garnished with eggs and parsley.

Caldeirada

Seafood Stew

Any type and selection of fish and seafood may be used in this dish.

Serves 6

½ cup (4 fl oz) olive oil

4 onions, sliced

2-4 cloves garlic (according to taste), crushed

5 tomatoes, peeled, seeded and chopped

3 sprigs parsley, chopped

2 bay leaves

salt

freshly ground black pepper

¼ teaspoon nutmeg

dash of Tabasco sauce

250 g (8 oz) of 3 types of fish fillets, cut into 2.5 cm (1-2 in) chunks

250 g (8 oz) squid, cleaned and cut into 5 x 2.5 cm (2 x 1 in) pieces

18 mussels

½ cup (4 fl oz) dry white wine

2 tablespoons vinegar

30 g (1 oz) melted butter

6 thick slices of bread, without crust

1. Preheat the oven to 180°C (350°F/Gas 4).
2. Heat the oil in a pan and sauté the onions and garlic until onions are soft and transparent.
3. Add tomatoes, parsley, bay leaves, salt, pepper, nutmeg and Tabasco, and simmer over low heat for 15 minutes.
4. In a heavy casserole, arrange layers of fish, squid and mussels alternating with the sauce.
5. Pour in wine, vinegar and butter, place the bread on top, cover the casserole, bring it to the boil on top of the stove.
6. Put it in the oven for 20 to 30 minutes. Serve hot from the casserole.

Escabeche

Pickled Fish

Serves 6

1 cup (8 fl oz) olive oil

1 kg (2 lb) white fish fillets

3 onions, sliced and separated into rings

2-4 cloves garlic (according to taste), crushed

3 carrots, coarsely grated

4 sprigs parsley, chopped

3 bay leaves

1 teaspoon paprika

¼ teaspoon chilli powder or dash of Tabasco sauce

1½ teaspoons salt

freshly ground black pepper

1 cup white wine vinegar

1. Heat half of the oil and fry the fish fillets. When they are cooked, remove the skin and any bones and break them up with a fork into large flakes.
2. Heat the rest of the oil and sauté the onion rings until soft and transparent.
3. Add the rest of the ingredients and cook for 5 minutes. Check seasoning.
4. Arrange the fish in a glass or glazed dish and pour the hot marinade over it. Cover the dish and refrigerate for 2 days.
5. Serve with sautéed potatoes.

Pastéis de Bacalhau

Codfish Cakes

Makes 6 flat, round cakes

500 g (1 lb) dried salt cod
2 cups (4 oz) soft breadcrumbs made
  from stale bread without crust
¾ cup (6 fl oz) olive oil
3 sprigs fresh coriander, finely
  chopped
4 sprigs parsley, finely chopped

4 mint leaves, finely chopped
2 tablespoons paprika
1 teaspoon salt
freshly ground black pepper
2-3 cloves garlic, each cut in two
6 freshly poached eggs

1. Soak the cod in cold water for 12 hours, changing water several times.
2. Place the cod in a saucepan, cover with water and simmer over low heat for 1 hour.
3. Drain, cool, remove skins and bones and, with a fork, flake it finely.
4. Soak the breadcrumbs in 6 tablespoons of oil.
5. In a bowl, combine the fish, coriander, parsley, mint, paprika, salt and pepper and the breadcrumbs. Thoroughly mix them together.
6. Divide the mixture into six. Dust your hands with flour and form the mixture into cakes about 10 cm (4 in) round and 2 cm (¾ in) thick.
7. Heat the remaining oil in a heavy frying pan and fry the garlic until golden brown. Discard them and fry the cakes in the oil for about 3 minutes on each side until brown.
8. Serve with a poached egg on each and garnished with parsley.

Atum à Algarvia

Tuna Steak with Wine and Bacon

Serves 4

1 tablespoon olive oil
125 g (4 oz) bacon, roughly chopped
750 g (1½ lb) fresh tuna, cut into
  steaks 3 cm (1¼ in) thick

2 onions, sliced
1 cup (8 fl oz) dry white wine
salt
freshly ground black pepper

1. Heat the oil in a pan and fry the bacon and onions until onions are soft and bacon starts to brown.
2. Add the tuna, and lightly fry on both sides.
3. Add the wine, and simmer over low heat for 10 minutes. Season, and serve with the bacon, onions and cooking juice poured over the tuna.

Right: The colourful bow of the richly painted boats of the Ria de Aveiro lagoon.

Camarão à Portuguêsa

Scampi or Prawn Skewers with Rice and Sauce

Serves 4

4 tablespoons olive oil
2 onions, finely chopped
3½ cups (21 oz) rice
7 cups (1.75 litres) fish stock
  (see p. 140)
salt
freshly ground black pepper

1 clove garlic, crushed
500 g (1 lb) tomatoes, peeled and
  chopped
½ cup (4 fl oz) dry white wine
12 olives, stoned
750 g (1½ lb) scampi or prawns

1. Heat 2 tablespoons of oil in a saucepan and sauté 1 chopped onion and the rice until they start to colour.
2. Add stock, and season. While stirring, bring to the boil, then cover and simmer over low heat for 20 minutes.
3. To make the sauce, heat 1 tablespoon of oil and sauté the remaining onion and the garlic until onion is soft and transparent. Add tomatoes, wine, olives and check seasoning.
4. Put the scampi or prawns on to skewers, brush them with the remaining tablespoon of oil and grill them for approximately 8 minutes.
5. To serve, dish out the rice on individual plates, place the skewers on top, and serve the sauce separately.

Lagosta à Portuguêsa

Lobster with Tomato and Brandy Sauce

Serves 2

1 onion, cut into quarters
3 sprigs parsley, roughly chopped
2 sprigs thyme, chopped
3 bay leaves
6 peppercorns
salt
1 fresh lobster or crayfish, cut into
  pieces
90 g (3 oz) butter

4 onions, finely chopped
1 clove garlic, crushed
500 g (1 lb) tomatoes, peeled and
  chopped
½ cup (4 fl oz) dry white wine
freshly ground black pepper
1 tablespoon flour
¼ cup (2 fl oz) brandy

1. In approximately 4 cups (1 litre) of water, simmer the onion quarters with parsley, thyme, bay leaves, peppercorns and salt for 15 minutes.
2. Place the lobster pieces in this stock, and simmer over low heat for 5 minutes. Set aside.
3. Melt 30 g of the butter and sauté the chopped onions and garlic until onions are soft.
4. Add tomatoes, wine, salt and pepper, rub through a sieve, and set aside.
5. In a saucepan, melt the remaining 60 g of butter, stir in the flour, and slowly add the hot tomato sauce, stirring until smooth. Simmer for 5 minutes.
6. Add the brandy and the lobster pieces, simmer for 4 minutes. Check seasoning. Serve with boiled rice or boiled potatoes.

Peixe Assado

Baked Fish with Port

Serves 4

2 tablespoons olive oil
2 onions, finely chopped
1 clove garlic, crushed
4 tomatoes, peeled, seeded and finely chopped
2 sprigs thyme, finely chopped

½ cup (4 fl oz) port
salt
freshly ground black pepper
4 plate-size snapper or other white-fleshed fish

1. Preheat the oven to 180°C (350°F/Gas 4).
2. Heat the oil and sauté onions and garlic until the onions are soft. Add tomatoes, thyme, port and seasoning.
3. Place the fish in a greased baking dish, pour the sauce over and bake in the preheated oven for 30 minutes. Serve the fish masked with the sauce.

Penteolas à Portuguêsa

Scallops with Pork, Tomatoes and Onions

Serves 6

2 tablespoons oil
1 onion, finely chopped
2 tomatoes, peeled, seeded and finely chopped
2 sprigs parsley, finely chopped
300 g (9⅔ oz) cooked pork, finely chopped
2-3 tablespoons flour
milk

12 scallops, chopped
salt
pepper
20 g (¾ oz) butter
6 scallop shells (for serving)
6 tablespoons dry breadcrumbs

1. Heat the oil and sauté the onion until golden.
2. Add tomatoes and parsley, and simmer for 30 minutes.
3. Rub through a sieve. Return to the saucepan, add pork and flour and cook for 3 minutes. Add enough milk and stir well until the mixture has a creamy consistency.
4. Add scallops, salt, pepper and butter, simmer for 2 minutes.
5. Place the mixture on the scallop shells, sprinkle with breadcrumbs, and place under a grill to brown.

Salada de Tuna e Amêndoas

Tuna and Almond Salad

Serves 4

2 tablespoons olive oil

500 g (1 lb) fresh tuna cut into slices 2.5 cm (1 in) thick (canned tuna may be used)

salt

freshly ground black pepper

½ cup (2 oz) seeded chopped black olives

2 hard-boiled eggs, chopped

¾ cup (3 oz) slivered blanched almonds

3 sticks celery, chopped

¾ cup (9 oz) mayonnaise (see p. 29)

juice 1 lemon

lettuce leaves (for serving)

1. Heat oil in pan and sauté the tuna for 3 minutes each side until cooked through. Season.
2. Cool the fish and break it up into flakes with a fork.
3. Mix it with the remaining ingredients, check seasoning, then serve on lettuce leaves.
4. If using canned tuna, drain it and mix it with the remaining ingredients.

Right: *View of the Castle of Braganca from Pousada S. Bartolomeu.*

Cherne à Portuguêsa

Baked Jewfish

*From **Casa de Leão**, Castelo de S. Jorge, Lisbon*

Serves 4

4 onions, sliced
1.5 kg (3 lb) jewfish (halibut)
salt
freshly ground pepper
1 clove garlic, crushed
1 cup (8 fl oz) dry white wine

1 tablespoon vinegar
2 tomatoes, peeled and sliced
2 bay leaves
4 cooked, sliced potatoes
3 tablespoons olive oil

1. Preheat the oven to 200°C (400°F/Gas 6).
2. Place half of the onion slices on the bottom of a buttered ovenproof dish.
3. Put the fish into the dish, sprinkle with salt, pepper, garlic, wine and vinegar.
4. Cover with the remaining onion slices, the tomatoes and bay leaves.
5. Arrange the potato slices around the fish. Sprinkle with olive oil and bake in the preheated oven for 45 minutes. Occasionally baste with the cooking juices.

Pargo Assado à Regional

Country-baked Red Porgy

*From **Pousada da Ria**, Torreira-Murtosa*

This dish is traditionally prepared in an ovenproof claypot. Any ovenproof dish may be used.

Serves 4-6

1 kg (2 lb) redfish fillets
salt
freshly ground pepper
2 onions, finely chopped
3 tomatoes, peeled and finely chopped

3 sprigs parsley, finely chopped
2 cloves garlic, crushed
1 cup (8 fl oz) dry white wine

1. Preheat the oven to 180°C (350°F/Gas 4).
2. Place the fish in a greased ovenproof dish and add remaining ingredients.
3. Bake in the preheated oven for 35 to 45 minutes, serve with boiled potatoes.

Ensopado de Congro à São Bartolomeu

Eel Fricassée with Egg-lemon Sauce

From **Pousada S. Bartolomeu**, *Bragança*

Serves 4

**1.25 kg (2½ lb) eel, skinned, boned
  and cut into 2 cm (¾ in) cubes**
salt
freshly ground pepper
2 tablespoons oil
1 onion, finely chopped
2 cloves garlic, crushed
2 bay leaves

1 cup (8 fl oz) milk
2 egg yolks, lightly beaten
juice 1-1½ lemons
8 trimmed slices of thin toast
3 sprigs parsley, chopped
lemon quarters for garnish

1. Sprinkle the eel with salt and pepper.
2. Heat the oil and sauté onion and garlic until onion is soft and transparent.
3. Add bay leaves, eel and milk, and simmer gently for a few minutes.
4. Reduce heat, and stir in egg yolks and lemon juice, season to taste. Heat until the sauce thickens, but do not boil.
5. Place the toast on a heated serving platter, ladle the eel and sauce on top, sprinkle with parsley and garnish with lemon wedges.

POULTRY AND GAMEBIRDS

Simplicity marks the preparation of most poultry dishes. Farmyard free-range chickens are still available and their natural flavour needs very little improvement.

I was introduced to Portugese chicken dishes in a small restaurant in the Alfama district of Lisbon. Marinated in a spicy lemon sauce, the chicken was simply grilled over glowing charcoal and was served with a tangy salad, washed down with a rough but tasty dry red wine.

Port wine is not used extensively in local cooking, and I suspect that recipes in which this delicious but expensive wine is used are of foreign origin, reimported into the country. Nevertheless, Portugese cooks do use this most famous of local wines and their dishes are really worth trying.

In season there are tasty gamebirds available and the simple local recipes bring out their natural flavour.

Frango na Pucana

Chicken Casserole with Port and Mustard

Serves 6

60 g (2 oz) butter	**¼ cup (2 fl oz) brandy**
2 tablespoons olive oil	**½ cup (4 fl oz) dry white wine**
1.5 kg (3 lb) chicken	**1 tablespoon mustard**
6 small onions, chopped	**125 g (4 oz) prosciutto-type ham, diced**
2 cloves garlic, crushed	**salt**
3 tomatoes, peeled and chopped	**freshly ground black pepper**
½ cup (4 fl oz) port	

1. Heat the butter and oil and brown the chicken all round. Put it in a casserole.
2. In the same fat, sauté onions and garlic until onions are golden brown.
3. Add tomatoes, port, brandy, wine and mustard, and simmer for 5 minutes. Add ham, season and pour it on top of the chicken in the casserole.
4. Cover, and simmer over low heat for 1 hour. Serve with fried potatoes.

Casa do Leão, Castelo de S. Jorge, Lisbon

From the high ramparts of the Castelo de São Jorge the view of Lisbon is most impressive. Just below the high walls is Alfama, a living reminder of its Moorish past. Narrow, twisting alleys and winding stairs, tiny open spaces and courtyards link clusters of houses into a confusing maze.

Towards the wide waters of the River Tagus is the elegant classical colonnaded Praça de Comercio, the symbolic gate to the city.

Casa do Leão is an elegant restaurant situated in the recently restored part of the Castelo de São Jorge. Here typical Portuguese dishes are offered to the guests, including Lombo de Porco Assado con Fruitas, roasted leg of pork with slices of fruit and grouper in the Portuguese manner.

After the meal a stroll about the ancient walls is very pleasant. Swans, wild ducks and other water birds inhabit the pools, while white peacocks proudly stride among the ruins.

Right: Some of the dishes served at Casa de Leao, Castelode Sao Jorge, Lisbon including bottom left: baked jewfish (p. 120).

Galinha de Fricassée

Chicken Fricassée

Serves 4-6

1.5 kg (3 lb) chicken, cut into pieces	salt
30 g (1 oz) butter	freshly ground black pepper
2 tablespoons oil	2 egg yolks, lightly beaten
1 cup (8 fl oz) dry white wine	1 sprig parsley, chopped
½ cup (4 fl oz) chicken stock (see p. 140)	juice 1 lemon
12 small onions	

1. Sauté the chicken pieces in butter and oil until golden brown.
2. Add wine, stock, onions, salt and pepper, cover the pan and simmer for 30 to 40 minutes until chicken is cooked.
3. Take out the chicken and keep it warm. Through a sieve, drain the liquid into a saucepan and whisk in the egg yolks, parsley and lemon juice. Season if necessary. While whisking continuously, heat it until the sauce thickens, but do not boil. To serve, place the chicken on a platter and pour the sauce over.

Galinha com Vinho do Pôrto

Chicken with Port Wine

Serves 4

1.5 kg (3 lb) chicken, cut into pieces	water
3 tablespoons olive oil	salt
2 onions, chopped	freshly ground pepper
2 sprigs parsley, chopped	1 tablespoon flour
1 cup (8 fl oz) port wine	triangular croûtons made from 4 slices of bread

1. Sauté the chicken in the oil, add onions and parsley, and fry until chicken is golden brown.
2. Transfer to a saucepan, add port wine and enough water to cover, season. Cover the pan and simmer over low heat until the chicken is cooked, about 30 minutes.
3. Thicken the cooking liquid with the flour mixed with a little cold water. Serve hot with the sauce and croûtons.

Perdiz Convento de Alcantara

Braised Stuffed Partridge with Port Alcantara

Ingredients are for 1 bird which will serve 2 people.

1 cup (2 oz) soft breadcrumbs
2 tablespoons oil
50 g (1¾ oz) liver pâté
2 tablespoons finely chopped pickled cucumbers
salt

freshly ground black pepper
1 partridge
½ cup (4 fl oz) port wine
½ cup (4 fl oz) dry white wine

1. Soak the breadcrumbs in the oil for 10 minutes.
2. In a bowl, combine breadcrumbs, pâté, pickles, salt and pepper. Mix well, and place the stuffing in the bird. Sew up the opening or secure it with skewers.
3. Place the bird in a bowl with the wines which have been seasoned. Cover and refrigerate for 24 hours, turning the bird occasionally.
4. Place the bird and the wine marinade in a heavy-lidded casserole, cover, bring to the boil and over low heat simmer for 1½ hours.
5. Remove the bird and reduce the sauce to half. To serve, cut the bird lengthways into two, making sure that the stuffing stays in the cavities. Arrange on a decorative platter, skin side up, and serve masked with the sauce.

Faisão Estufado

Stewed Pheasant with Brandy, Port and Almonds

Serves 6

2 pheasants
salt
freshly ground black pepper
¾ cup (6 fl oz) brandy
¾ cup (6 fl oz) port

90 g (3 oz) butter
12 blanched almonds
12 small onions
4 sprigs fresh thyme and/or oregano, chopped

1. Season the pheasants and marinate them in brandy and port for 2 days. Turn them occasionally.
2. In the butter, fry the pheasants with almonds and onions until golden brown.
3. Transfer them to a casserole, add the marinade, cover the casserole, and over low heat simmer for 1 to 1½ hours until the pheasants are tender.
4. Season if necessary. If desired, the cooking juices may be thickened with a little flour. Cut each bird into 6 pieces, arrange on a serving platter and pour the sauce, almonds and onions over. Serve hot.

MEATS

Portuguese meat dishes are rather simple yet full of flavour and they reflect their peasant origin. The local cooks are at their best when they prepare a tasty stew. Cozido à Portuguêsa is the quintessence of such a stew, where shin beef, bacon and vegetables combine with spicy chouriço sausage and rice. There are many local versions of this Cozido.

Pork is popular throughout the country; and as is becoming for a fishing nation, there is even a dish where pork and mussels are combined.

The Portuguese people are fond of tripe and the two best-known dishes are the Tripas à Moda from Oporto and the Dobrada com Grão from Lisbon. Liver is moist and tender when marinated in dry white wine and briefly fried in oil.

In general, there is very little grazing land in the country and Portuguese culinary fame still rests on its seafood.

Portuguese Steak

Serves 8

60 g (2 oz) butter	**1 tablespoon vinegar**
4 onions, sliced	**1 sprig parsley, chopped**
1 clove garlic, crushed	**salt**
4 tomatoes, peeled, seeded and chopped	**freshly ground black pepper**
1 tablespoon tomato purée	**8 rump steaks**

1. Melt the butter and sauté onions and garlic until onions are soft and transparent.
2. Add tomatoes, tomato purée, vinegar, parsley, salt and pepper. Simmer for 20 minutes.
3. Grill the steak to your liking. To serve, pour the sauce over the steaks and garnish with parsley, and serve with boiled or fried potatoes.

Pousada de Oliveira, Guimarães

Guimarães is the cradle of the Portuguese nation. The 10th-century castle, where Alfonso Henriques, the first Portuguese king lived, looks down on this picturesque town. Many 14th and 15th century churches and houses of the nobility can be found along the winding streets.

The Pousada de Oliveira is situated in an ancient square, in a former mansion which has been skilfully restored to preserve the old world atmosphere. In pleasant surroundings, good traditional regional food is served. As in most restaurants throughout Portugal, bacalhau, the dried cod, is cooked in many different and tasty ways.

There is also the inevitable Caldo Verde, the national green soup made from kale; today eaten throughout the country, it originated in this region.

The vinho verde produced in these northern regions of Portugal is ever present. Refreshing and light, with its subtle characteristic effervescence, the wine is a welcome accompaniment to local dishes.

Right: Three of the house specialities of Pousada de Oliveira, Guimarães including bottom right: caldo verde soup.

Cozido à Portuguêsa

Portuguese Meat Stew and Rice

Serves 6-8

1 kg (2 lb) shin beef
250 g (8 oz) smoked bacon
1 kg (2 lb) potatoes, cut into quarters
500 g (1 lb) carrots, thickly sliced
500 g (1 lb) turnips, thickly sliced

1 large cabbage, cut into quarters
250 g (8 oz) chouriço (spicy pork sausage), sliced
salt
2 cups (12 oz) rice

1. Place the beef and bacon in a large saucepan of boiling water and simmer over low heat for 2 hours.
2. Add potatoes, carrots, turnips and cabbage. After 15 minutes of cooking add chouriço sausage.
3. Remove 4 cups (1 litre) of liquid and place in a separate saucepan. In this, cook the rice, under cover, undisturbed for 20 minutes; the rice should absorb most of the liquid. During that time, continue to simmer meat and vegetables. When cooked, if necessary adjust the seasoning.
4. Serve the liquid as a soup. In accordance with tradition, serve the meat and vegetables arranged in separate mounds on a very large platter, accompanied by the rice.

Ensopada de Borrego

Stewed Lamb with Onions

Serves 4-6

1 kg (2 lb) lamb, cut into cubes
flour
125 g (4 oz) lard
500 g (1 lb) onions, sliced
4 cloves garlic, crushed
2 bay leaves
1 tablespoon crushed peppercorns

salt
pinch of hot chilli
1 tablespoon paprika
2 sprigs parsley, chopped
3 tablespoons vinegar
8-12 slices of stale bread

1. Dust the meat with flour. In a frying pan, fry it in half of the lard until golden. Put the meat in a casserole.
2. Melt the rest of the lard in the frying pan and sauté onions, garlic, bay leaves and pepper until onions are soft and transparent. Add them to the casserole.
3. Add salt, chilli, paprika, parsley, vinegar and approximately 4 cups (1 litre) water. Cover the casserole, bring to the boil and simmer over low heat for 1½ hours until lamb is tender.
4. To serve, place the bread into large soup bowls and pour the hot broth on top. Serve the rest separately.

Posta de Vitela à Transmontana

Marinated Roast Veal

From **Pousada S. Bartolomeu**, *Bragança*

Serves 6

2 cups (16 fl oz) dry white wine
2 cloves garlic, crushed
1 tablespoon paprika
¼ cup (2 fl oz) olive oil
salt
freshly ground pepper

1.5 kg (3 lb) rolled veal shoulder
1½ cups (12 fl oz) water
2 tablespoons vinegar
3 tablespoons finely chopped mixed
  pickles

1. Combine wine, garlic, paprika, oil, salt and pepper and marinate the meat for two days, turn occasionally.
2. Preheat the oven to 180°C (350°F/Gas 4).
3. Roast the meat on a rack placed in a roasting dish for 1½ to 2 hours. Occasionally baste with the marinade. When cooked, keep the meat warm.
4. Pour the remaining marinade and cooking juices into a saucepan, add water, vinegar and pickles and boil rapidly to reduce to 2 cups (16 fl oz). Season to taste.
5. Serve the meat cut into slices with a little of the sauce poured over it. Serve the rest of the sauce separately. Traditionally the veal is served with baked potatoes and a vegetable, especially spinach purée, cooked with garlic and oil.

Vitela Assada

Roast Veal with Tomatoes and Onions

Serves 4

4 slices prosciutto-type ham
4 thick veal chops
6 tomatoes, peeled, seeded and
  chopped
2 onions, sliced

salt
freshly ground black pepper
1 cup (8 fl oz) port

1. Preheat the oven to 180°C (350°F/Gas 4).
2. Place a slice of ham on each chop and place them in an oven dish.
3. Cover the chops with tomatoes and onions, sprinkle with salt and pepper, and pour the port over.
4. Cook in the preheated oven for 1 to 1¼ hours or until meat is tender. Serve directly from the oven dish.

Vitela Assada no Espeto

Basting Mixture for Roast Veal

In the original dish which came from the northern provence of Trás-os-Montes, the veal is spit roasted.

¼ cup (2 fl oz) olive oil
1 teaspoon vinegar
2 cloves garlic, crushed

2 sprigs parsley, finely chopped
1 teaspoon finely chopped hot chilli
freshly ground black pepper

1. Mix all ingredients and let them stand for 2 to 3 hours for the flavours to blend.
2. Baste meat with mixture while roasting it slowly in a low oven.

Lombo de Porco de Monção

Spicy Loin of Pork

Serves 4

1 kg (2 lb) loin of pork
½ cup (4 fl oz) dry white wine
4 cloves
¼ teaspoon nutmeg
1 bay leaf

salt
freshly ground black pepper
16-20 roasted, peeled chestnuts (optional)

1. Preheat the oven to 180°C (350°F/Gas 4).
2. Put the meat in a roasting dish with the wine, cloves, nutmeg, bay leaf, salt and pepper.
3. Place the dish in the preheated oven and cook for 1½ hours, basting the meat frequently.
4. Degrease the cooking juices, season and serve with the sliced meat which can be garnished with chestnuts.

Right: Market Cross, Guimarães.

Costeletas de Porco à Alentejana

Pork Cutlets with Green Pepper Paste

Serves 4

8 pork cutlets
2 cloves garlic, crushed
salt
freshly ground black pepper
1 tablespoon green pepper (capsicum)
  paste (see p. 141)

3 tablespoons dry white wine
1 egg, lightly beaten with 2
  tablespoons water
½ cup (2 oz) dry breadcrumbs
oil for deep frying
16 orange slices

1. Rub the cutlets with a mixture of garlic, salt, pepper and green pepper paste.
2. Place them in a flat dish and add the wine. Cover with plastic film and refrigerate for 24 hours. Occasionally spoon the liquid over the chops.
3. Dip the chops in the egg mixture and the breadcrumbs, and deep fry until golden brown.
4. Serve hot, garnished with orange slices.

Carne de Porco à Alentejana

Pork and Mussels

Serves 4

500 g (1 lb) lean pork, cut into small
  pieces
30 g (1 oz) lard
1 tablespoon olive oil
2 onions chopped
2 tomatoes, peeled and chopped

2 bay leaves
salt
freshly ground black pepper
1 tablespoon paprika
500 g (1 lb) mussels

1. Fry the pork in the lard until the meat is almost cooked. Set aside.
2. Heat the oil and sauté onions until soft and transparent. Add tomatoes, bay leaves, salt, pepper and paprika for 10 minutes.
3. Add mussels and the pork, and cook until mussels open. Serve hot with crusty bread.

Lombo Assado à Alentejana

Roast Loin of Pork

Serves 4

1 kg (2 lb) loin of pork
2 cloves garlic, crushed
1 tablespoon green pepper (capsicum)
  paste (see p. 141)

salt
freshly ground black pepper
½ cup (4 fl oz) dry white wine
½ cup (4 fl oz) water

1. Preheat the oven to 180°C (350°F /Gas 4).
2. Mix the garlic, green pepper paste, salt and pepper and spread it over the meat.
3. Put it in a roasting dish, add wine, water, salt and pepper. Place the dish in the preheated oven and roast it for 1½ hours until the meat is done. If necessary, add more wine or water.
4. Degrease the cooking juices and serve the meat slices masked with the gravy.

Iscas à Portuguêsa

Marinated Fried Liver

Serves 4

500 g (1 lb) calf's liver (can be pig's or
  lamb's), thinly sliced
1 cup (8 fl oz) dry white wine
1 clove garlic, crushed
2 cloves
6 crushed peppercorns

2 bay leaves
salt
flour
2 rashers bacon, chopped
2 tablespoons olive oil
3 potatoes, peeled and finely diced

1. Marinate the liver in a mixture of wine, garlic, cloves, peppercorns, bay leaves and salt. Refrigerate overnight.
2. Take the liver out of the marinade. Heat the marinade to reduce it by half.
3. Pat the liver dry, dust it with flour, and fry it briefly in the oil with the bacon and potatoes. Serve it with the reduced marinade.

DESSERTS AND CAKES

Most desserts, sweets and cakes in Portugal are very sweet and that's the way they like them. Yet like their Spanish neighbours, Portuguese people prefer to finish off their meal with fresh fruit in season.

Among the sweet and lush desserts, those made from egg yolks are the most numerous and indeed the most popular. Rich, creamy and thick in texture, the custard in various forms and guises reigns supreme. Its crowning glory, Portugal's national dessert, is the caramel custard, the Pudim flan.

Not less popular and frequently used are the Ovos Moles, an egg yolk and sugar mixture which is either formed into various shapes or used as a filling for other confectionary preparations. Ovos Moles originated in Aveiro and the best-known sweets of this type come from there.

Marzipan is popular and it is a legacy of Moorish days. Nuts and dried fruit, especially figs which are grown in the southern part of the country, are an important ingredient of many desserts. From the days of Portuguese exploration in the Orient, today's cooks have inherited a taste for spices such as cinnamon, cloves and nutmeg.

The Portuguese prefer their cakes rich and sweet, with the main ingredients being eggs, sugar and almonds and sometimes honey.

Preserved fruit and especially quinces add to a very rich repertoire to satisfy the sweetest palate.

Ovos Moles

Serves 4

1 cup (8 oz) sugar	**6 egg yolks**
½ cup (4 fl oz) water	

1. Boil the sugar and the water to make a light syrup.
2. Allow it to cool.
3. Beat the egg yolks until they are creamy, and gradually add the syrup.
4. Pour the mixture into the saucepan and slowly heat, stirring it constantly until it thickens. Do not boil.
5. Pour it into a bowl, cool it, place it into the refrigerator and serve it when chilled.

Right: Display of fresh fruit at Pousada de Oliveira, Guimarães.

Almond Pudding with Port

Serves 4-6

2¼ cups (8 oz) ground almonds
1¼ cups (10 fl oz) milk, boiling
1 cup (8 oz) sugar
½ cup (4 fl oz) port

3 eggs
3 egg whites
3 tablespoons sugar

1. Combine almonds, boiling milk, sugar and port, and let it stand for 10 minutes.
2. Whip the eggs and egg whites together and gently stir them into the mixture.
3. Sprinkle the sugar on the bottom of a flameproof mould and place it over heat until it melts and browns. Do not burn it, as it will then be bitter. Cool it until it sets.
4. Pour the mixture into the mould. Cover it and place it in a pan with water. Heat the pan and steam the mould until the mixture sets. Leave it to cool, and unmould it to serve.

Mousse de Ananás

Pineapple Mousse

Serves 4-6

3 tablespoons (1 oz) cornflour
   (cornstarch)
2¾ cups (22 fl oz) milk
6 egg yolks, well beaten

400 g (13 oz) canned pineapple with
   juice
sugar (optional)

1. Mix the cornflour and milk. While stirring, boil it until the mixture thickens.
2. Add the beaten egg yolks, stir it over low heat, do not boil.
3. Add finely chopped pineapple and 2 or 3 tablespoons of the pineapple juice. Taste it, and if necessary add some sugar, stir the mixture to dissolve the sugar.
4. Pour it into a serving dish and refrigerate. Serve with sweetened fresh or whipped cream.

Morangos com Vinho do Pôrto

Strawberries and Oranges with Port

Serves 4

250 g (8 oz) strawberries, hulled
½ cup (4 fl oz) port wine
2 oranges, peeled and thinly sliced
2 tablespoons sugar

½ cup (4 fl oz) cream, whipped with
   1 teaspoon sugar and ½ teaspoon
   vanilla essence

1. Soak the strawberries with the port for 30 minutes.
2. Add the orange slices, sugar to taste, and refrigerate for 1 hour.
3. Serve with the cream.

Pudim Madeira

Madeira Pudding

Serves 4

2 tablespoons sugar dissolved in
  2 tablespoons water
1 cup (8 oz) sugar
1 tablespoon vinegar
2 eggs

6 egg yolks
1¾ cups (14 fl oz) milk, hot
¼ cup (2 fl oz) Madeira or port

1. Dissolve the sugar-water mixture over low heat, and cook over moderate heat until the mixture turns light amber colour. Pour this caramel into a pudding mould to coat the bottom and sides.
2. In a bowl, combine the sugar, vinegar, eggs and egg yolks, and beat with a whisk until the sugar dissolves and the mixture is pale yellow.
3. Slowly add the hot milk and the Madeira or port. Pour the mixture into the caramel-lined mould. Place the mould in a pan with water, cover it and bake in the preheated oven for 45 minutes to 1 hour, until it sets.
4. Allow it to cool and then refrigerate it. To serve, unmould it on to a decorative plate.

Pudim de Bananas

Light Banana Soufflé

Serves 4

6 bananas, finely sliced
5 tablespoons sugar
juice ½ lemon

½ cup (4 fl oz) port
6 egg whites
½ teaspoon vanilla essence

1. Preheat the oven to 180°C (350°F /Gas 4).
2. Butter a soufflé mould and sprinkle it with a little sugar.
3. Mix the bananas with 2 tablespoons sugar, lemon juice and port.
4. Put them into the mould.
5. Whip the egg whites with the remaining 3 tablespoons of sugar and the vanilla essence to a glossy meringue.
6. Spoon it on top of the bananas and bake in the preheated oven for 20 to 30 minutes. Serve immediately.

Torta de Laranja

Orange Roll

From **Pousada S. Bartolomeu,** *Bragança*

10 eggs
2 cups (1 lb) sugar
2 tablespoons flour

1 cup (8 fl oz) fresh orange juice
orange slices and cherries in syrup for garnish

1. Preheat the oven to 200°C (400°F /Gas 6).
2. Beat the eggs with sugar until they are light and the sugar has dissolved.
3. Mix in the flour, and slowly incorporate the orange juice.
4. Pour the mixture into a shallow greased baking tray, sprinkled with flour.
5. Bake in the preheated oven for 30 minutes or until the mixture sets.
6. Let it cool. Form it into a roll, slice it and serve it with orange slices and cherries in syrup.

Arroz doce

Portuguese Sweet Rice

From **Pousada de S. Lourenço,** *Manteigas, Serra da Estrela*

Serves 6

1 cup (6½ oz) rice
salt
2 cups (16 fl oz) water
2 cups (16 fl oz) milk
1 teaspoon vanilla essence

1 teaspoon cinnamon
thin slivers of lemon rind
3 egg yolks
½ cup (4 oz) sugar

1. Cook the rice covered in salted water for 15 to 20 minutes until all moisture is absorbed and the rice is cooked.
2. Fluff the rice up with a fork, and let it stand for 10 minutes.
3. Combine milk, vanilla, cinnamon and lemon rind, and simmer it for 10 minutes.
4. Remove from heat, and let it stand for 10 minutes. Remove lemon rind.
5. Cream the egg yolks with the sugar until sugar is dissolved and the mixture is pale yellow. Gradually add the spiced milk.
6. Pour the mixture into a saucepan and over low heat stir constantly until the custard thickens. Do not boil.
7. Add the rice, leave it over low heat while continuing to stir for 2 to 3 minutes, until rice heats up. To serve pour the rice into a glass serving bowl or individual dessert dishes. Sprinkle the top with cinnamon and serve at room temperature.

Right: Cork trees. When the cork bark is removed the tree turns a brilliant orange colour. It takes 9 years for the bark to re-grow.

BASIC RECIPES
Fish Stock

Makes approximately 1¾ cups (14 fl oz)

1 kg (2 lb) fish trimmings, such as fish heads, bones, fresh or cooked shellfish leftovers
1 onion, thinly sliced
6-8 parsley stems (not the leaves; they will darken the stock)

1 teaspoon lemon juice
¼ teaspoon salt
1 cup (8 fl oz) dry white wine
cold water to cover

1. Place all the ingredients in a large heavy saucepan.
2. Bring it to the boil, skim, and simmer gently for 30 minutes.
3. Strain the stock through a fine sieve and correct the seasoning.
4. Fish stock may be refrigerated or deep frozen.

Chicken Stock

Makes 10 cups (2.5 litres)

1.5 kg (3 lb) boiling chicken with giblets
8-12 cups (2-3 litres) water
2 carrots, sliced
1 turnip, sliced
3 stalks celery, sliced

2 onions, unpeeled and halved
½ bunch parsley, roughly chopped
1 sprig thyme, chopped
6 peppercorns
3 bay leaves

1. In a large saucepan combine all the ingredients, making certain that the heart, stomach and liver have been properly cleaned.
2. Bring slowly to the boil and continue to simmer over low heat for 2 to 2½ hours.
3. Let all the ingredients cool in the stock, then strain, refrigerate and degrease it.
4. Discard the vegetables but keep the chicken. Remove the meat from the bones. It can be either chopped and used in a chicken soup or minced and made into chicken croquettes.
5. Use the stock in the preparation of soups and sauces. It may be refrigerated and will keep for 3 to 4 days or frozen when it may be kept for months.

Beef Stock

Meat stock is very useful in the preparation of soups and sauces; the quantity given here may seem excessive, but it can be deep frozen and kept at hand for future use.

Makes 16 cups (4 litres)

2 kg (4 lb) shin beef on the bone
2 kg (4 lb) veal knuckle (cut into 5 cm (2 in) pieces)
4 pigs' trotters
2 kg (4 lb) veal and beef bones (preferably marrow bones, sawn into pieces)
60 g (2 oz) dripping

2 cups carrots, chopped
2 cups onions, chopped
1½ cups celery, chopped
1 bouquet garni of parsley, thyme, marjoram
4 bay leaves
12 black peppercorns
24 cups (6 litres) water

1. In a large saucepan, place all ingredients, except the bouquet garni, peppercorns and water and cook gently, stirring occasionally, until the meat, bones and vegetables have browned slightly.
2. Add the bouquet garni and peppercorns.
3. Add the water and slowly bring to the boil.
4. Simmer 6 to 8 hours until the liquid is reduced to 16 cups (4 litres).
5. Cool and strain through muslin. Skim off the fat by refrigerating the liquid overnight and removing the congealed fat the next day.

Capsicum Paste

Green Pepper Paste

This is a method of preserving red or green peppers (capsicums) and is used for coating meats.

12 red or green peppers (capsicums), seeded and cut into pieces
3 thin slices of fresh ginger
2 onions, cut into quarters

salt
2 tablespoons olive oil

1. Combine all ingredients, except oil, in a food processor and process until a fine texture.
2. Place it in a jar, cover with oil and refrigerate for several days before using. It will keep for a long time.

INDEX
SPAIN